MISCELLANEOUS
PIECES

OF

Antient ENGLISH POESIE.

VIZ.

The Troublefome Raigne of King JOHN,

Written by SHAKESPEARE,

Extant in no Edition of his Writings.

The Metamorphofis of PIGMALION's Image, and certain Satyres.

By JOHN MARSTON.

The SCOURGE of VILLANIE. By the fame.

All printed before the YEAR 1600.

LONDON:

rinted for ROBERT HORSEFIELD, at the Crown in Ludgate-Street.

This scarce antiquarian book is included in our special *Legacy Reprint Series*. In the interest of creating a more extensive selection of rare historical book reprints, we have chosen to reproduce this title even though it may possibly have occasional imperfections such as missing and blurred pages, missing text, poor pictures, markings, dark backgrounds and other reproduction issues beyond our control. Because this work is culturally important, we have made it available as a part of our commitment to protecting, preserving and promoting the world's literature. Thank you for your understanding.

PREFACE.

IT may not be amiss to premise a few words respecting the several poems now offered to the publick: that deference is due to them who are to judge of the merit or taste of the fare that is set before them. Without farther preamble let us come to the first piece, the first work probably of the great man whose name it bears, and whose genuine performance it most unquestionably is. 'Tis somewhat remarkable that the several editors of *Shakespeare* should have so totally

A 2   tally

PREFACE.

tally unnoticed this work, as not to have told their readers that it contains nothing to be met with in any of their several editions. *Theobald* and *Warburton* have given us the title in their several lifts of his Writings, but make no mention of this particular.---It has been the fubject of much fpeculation, which was the firft production of this great and fingular genius, but hitherto nothing feems afcertained on this Head. However, thus far is indifputable, that this is his earlieft publication, and the only one of the year in which it was publifhed. 'Tis more than probable fome years elapfed before he publifhed any thing elfe: the author of the Britifh Theatre, Lond. 1752, is by no means to be relied on in his dates.---Sir *John Harington* in his

PREFACE.

in his apology of poetry, of the
year 1591, mentions the acting of
a tragedy of King Richard III. at
Cambridge, but does not even
hint at the author; so that cannot
be supposed to interfere with the
precedence of this. We may ob-
serve that *Shakespeare* varied and
curtailed his plan in the play, as it
now stands in the several editions
of his writings.---The present work
will be found to contain many
speeches worthy of its author: and
there is much singular humour in
those of the bastard; particularly
in the ballad-metre-dialogue betwixt him and the friar. But it is
not the province of an editor to
anticipate: a word or two however, concerning the British Persius *John Marston*, may not be
unuseful. Of him very little is

recorded

recorded with certainty. *Antony a Wood*, who is generally exact in his accounts of men, and much to be relied upon, is remarkably deficient with respect to him; indeed there seems to be little reason to think he was of Oxford: it is certain from his works that he was of Cambridge, where he was cotempary with Mr. *Hall*, with whom, as it appears from his satyre, called Reactio, and from the Scourge of Villanie, sat. 10. he had some dispute. To say any thing of the latter will be superfluous, as every reader has an opportunity of perusing that: the former it may not be amiss to canvass. And here it must be observed that *Hall's* Satyres, though of late they have been much the subject of encomium, yet antiently

they

PREFACE.

they were not in very high esteem, as will appear from the ridicule of *Marston*, and from the very severe criticism which *Milton* has on them in his apology for *Smectymnuus*, Sect. vi. But let us hear *Marston's* parodies of *Hall*.

Marston, p. 151.
Come daunce ye ftumbling Satyres by his fide.
Hall, *defiance to envy*, Stanza xvii.
Come dance ye nimble Driads by my fide.
Marston, 155.
Speake ye attentive Swaines that heard him never.
Hall, ib. Stanza xviii.
Speake ye attentive Swaines that heard me late.

And indeed almoft all the Italick lines, p. 155, are allufions to the fame piece : and particularly thefe fubfequent ones refer to the firft ftanzas of the above; and to the epithet he gave himfelf to his fa-tyres:

Envie,

PREFACE.

Envie, let pines of Ida reft alone,
For they will grow fpight of the thunder ftone,
Strive not to nibble in their fwelling graine
With *tootblefs gums* of thy detracting braine.

It has not been generally known who was the author of Pigmalion and the five fatyres: but that they belong to *Marfton* is clear from the fixth and tenth fatyres of the Scourge of Villanie: and to this may be added the evidence of the collector of England's Parnaffus, printed 1600, who cites the five firft lines of the dedication to opinion, prefixed to Pigmalion by the name of *I. Marfton*, p. 221. Why and whence he took the adopted Name of *Kinfayder*, it will be to little purpofe to guefs: that he was known by it to his cotemporaries, appears from a paffage in the Return from Parnaffus, Act i. fc. ii.

Fitz-

PREFACE.

Fitz-Geoffry has fix verfes to him in his *Affaniæ*, l. 2, which as the book is not in every one's poffef-fion, are here inferted.

Ad IOHANNEM MARSTONIUM.

Gloria MARSTONI fatyrarum proximâ primæ,
    Primaque, fas primas fi numerare duas;
Sin primam duplicare nefas, tu gloria faltem
    MARSTONI primæ proxima femper eris.
Nec te pæniteat ftationis, IANE, fecundus
    Cum duo fint tantum, eft neuter, at ambo
    pares.

Thefe fatyres, fays Mr. *Warton* in his obfervations on *Spenfer*, contain many well drawn characters and feveral good ftrokes of a faty-rical genius, but are not upon the whole fo finifhed and claffical as Bifhop *Hall's:* the truth is they were fatyrifts of a different caft: *Hall* turned his pen againft his co-tempo-

PREFACE.

temporary writers, and particularly verfifiers, *Marſton* chiefly in-
veighed againſt the growing foibles
and vices of the age. Nothing
remains but to obferve, that the
prefent edition of the Scourge of
Villanie is carefully printed from
the fecond, and that the tenth
fatyre was not in the firſt.

THE

FIRST AND SECOND PART

Of the troublefome RAIGNE of

JOHN KING of ENGLAND,

With the DISCOVERY of

King RICHARD CORDELION's bafe Sonne

(Vulgarly named the Baftard Fauconbridge:)

ALSO,

The Death of King JOHN at Swinftead Abbey.

As they were (fundry times) lately acted by the Queenes Majefties Players.

Written by W. Sh.

Imprinted at London by *Valentine Simmes* for *John Helme,* and are to be fold at his fhop in Saint Dunftons Churchyard in Fleeteftreet.

1 6 1 1.

Reprinted in the Year 1 7 6 4.

Dramatis Perſonæ.

KING John.
   Prince Henry his Son.
Arthur Duke of Brittaine.
Philip King of France.
Lewis the Dauphin.
Limoges Duke of Auſtria.
Earl of Pembroke,
———— Eſſex,
———— Saliſbury,
———— Cheſter,
———— Clare,
Lord Bewchampe,
Hubert de Burgh. } Engliſh Lords.
Earl Bigot,
Viſcount Meloun, } French Lords.
Chattilion the French Embaſſadour.
Robert Fauconbridge.
Phillip the Baſtard, otherwiſe Sir Philip Plantagenet.
Shrive of Northamtonſhire.
Pandulpho the Pope's Legate.
Peter of Pomfret, a Prophet.
Abbot of Swinſtead, Two Monks, Two Friars of the
   ſame, Two Franciſcan Friars, Citizens of Angiers,
   Heralds, &c.

Elinor, Queen Mother of England.
Conſtance, Dutcheſs Dowager of Britaine, Mother of
   Arthur.
Blanch, Niece to King John, married to the Dauphin
   Lewis.
Lady Margaret Fauconbridge.
A Nunne.

   Scene moſtly in England, ſometimes in France.

THE

Troublefome RAIGNE

OF

KING IOHN.

Enter K. Iohn, *Queene* Elianor *his Mother,* William Mar-
fhall, *Earle of* Pembrooke, *the Earles of* Effex, *and
of* Salifbury.

Queene Elianor.

BArons of *England,* and my noble Lords;
Though God and Fortune haue bereft from vs
Victorious *Richard,* fcourge of Infidells,
And clad this Land in ftole of difmall hew:
Yet giue me leaue to ioy, and ioy you all,
That from this wombe hath fprung a fecond hope,
A King that may in rule and vertue both
Succeede his brother in his Emperie.
    K. Iohn. My gratious mother Queene, and Barons all;
Though farre vnworthy of fo high a place,

B   A4

As is the Throne of mighty *Englands* King;
Yet *Iohn* your Lord, contented vncontent,
Will (as he may) suftaine the heauy yoke
Of preffing cares, that hang vpon a Crowne.
My Lord of *Pembrooke* and Lord *Salisbury*,
Admit the Lord *Chattilion* to our presence;
That we may know what *Philip* King of *Fraunce*
(By his Ambaffadors) requires of vs.

   Q. Elianor. Dare lay my hand that *Elianor* can geffe
Whereto this weighty Embaffade doth tend :
If of my nephew *Arthur* and his claime,
Then fay, my Sonne, I haue not miffde my aime.

      Enter Chattilion *and the two Earles.*

   K. Iohn. My Lord *Chattilion*, welcome into *England*:
How fares our Brother *Philip* King of *Fraunce* ?
   Chat. His Highneffe at my comming was in health,
And will'd me to falute your Maieftie,
And fay the meffage he hath giuen in charge.
   K. Iohn. And fpare not man, wee are preparde to heare.
   Chat. Philip, by the grace of God, moft Chriftian
King of *Fraunce*, hauing taken into his gardain and pro-
tection *Arthur* D. of *Britaine*, fonne and heire to *Ieffrey*
thine elder brother, requireth in the behalfe of the faide
Arthur, the kingdome of *England*, with the lordfhip of
Ireland, Poiters, Aniow, Teraine, Maine: and I attend
thine anfwer.
   K. Iohn. A fmall requeft : belike hee makes account,
That *England, Ireland, Poiters, Aniow, Toraine, Maine,*
Are nothing for a King to giue at once:
I wonder what he meanes to leaue for me.

                              Tell

Tell *Philip*, he may keepe his Lords at home,
With greater honour than to send them thus
On Embaſſades that not concerne himſelfe,
Or if they did, would yeeld but ſmall returne.

   Chat. Is this thine anſwer?

   K. Iohn. It is, and too good an anſwer for ſo prowd a meſſage.

   Chat. Then King of *England*, in my Máſters name,
And in Prince *Arthur* Duke of *Britaints* name,
I do defie thee as an enemie,
And wiſh thee to prepare for bloody warres.

   Q. Elianor. My Lord (that ſtands vpon defiance thus)
Commend me to my nephew, tell the boy,
That I Queen *Elianor* (his grandmother)
Vpon my bleſſing charge, him leaue his Armes,
Whereto his head-ſtrong mother prickes him ſo:
Her pride we knew, and know her for a Dame
That will not ſticke to bring him to his end,
So ſhe may bring her ſelfe to rule a realme.
Next, wiſh him to forſake the King of *Fraunce*,
And come to me and to his vncle here,
And he ſhall want for nothing at our hands.

   Chat. This ſhall I do, and thus I take my leaue.

   K. Iohn. Pembrooke, connaey him ſafely to the ſea,
But not in haſte: for as we are aduiſde,
We meane to be in *Fraunce* as ſoone as he,
To fortifie ſuch townes as we poſſeſſe
In *Aniow*, *Toraine*, and in *Normandie.*   [*Exit* Chatt.

B 2   *Enter*

Enter the Shriue and whispers the Earle of Salisbury *in the eare.*

Salf. Pleafe it your maiefty, here is the Shriue of Northamptonfhire, with certaine perfons that of late committed a riot, and haue appeald to your Maieftie, befeeching your Highneffe for fpeciall caufe to heare them.   (caufe,

K. Iohn. Will them come neere, and whilewee heare the
Goe *Salifbury* and make prouifion,
We meane with fpeed to paffe the Sea to *Fraunce.*
Say Shriue, what are thefe men, what haue they done?
Or whereto tends the eourfe of this appeale?

Shriue. Pleafe it your Maieftie, thefe two brethren vnnaturally falling at odds about their fathers liuing, haue broken your highneffe peace, in feeking to right their owne wrongs without courfe of Lawe, or order of Iuftice; and unlawfully affembled themfelues in mutinous maner, hauing committed a riot, appealing from triall in their country to your Highnes; and here I *Thomas Nidigate* Shriue of Northamptonfhire do deliuer them ouer to their triall.

K. Iohn. My Lord of *Effex*, will thoffenders to ftand forth, and tell the caufe of their quarrell.

Effex. Gentlemen, it is the Kings pleafure that you difcouer your griefs, and doubt not but you fhal haue iuftice.

Phil. Pleafe it your Maiefty the wrong is mine: yet will I abide all wrongs, before I once open my mouth t'vnrip the fhamefull flander of my parents, the difhonor

of

of my felf, and the bad dealing of my brother in this
princely affemblie.

 Robert. Then, by my Prince his leaue, fhall *Robert*
And tell your Maieftie what right I haue   (fpeake,
To offer wrong, as he accounteth wrong.
My father (not vnknowne vnto your Grace)
Receiu'd his fpurres of Knighthood in the Field,
At kingly *Richards* hands in *Paleftine*,
Whenas the walls of *Acon* gaue him way:
His name fir *Robert Fauconbridge* of *Mountbery*.
What by fucceffion from his Anceftors,
And warlike feruice vnder *Englands* Armes,
His liuing did amount to at his death
Two thoufand markes reuenew euery yeare:
And this (my Lord) I challenge for my right,
As lawfull heire to *Robert Fauconbridge*.

 Philip. If firft-borne fonne be heire indubitate
By certaine right of *Englands* auntient Lawe,
How fhould my felfe make any other doubt,
But I am heire to *Robert Fauconbridge?*

 K. Iohn. Fond youth, to trouble thefe our princely
Or make a queftion in fo plaine a cafe: (eares,
Speake; is this man thine elder brother borne?

 Robert. Pleafe it your Grace with patience for to heare,
I not deny but he mine elder is,
Mine elder brother too: yet in fuch fort,
As he can make no title to the land.

 K. Iohn. A doubtfull tale as euer I did heare,
Thy brother, and thine elder, and no heire:
Explaine this darke *Enigma*.

 Robert. I grant (my Lord) he is my mothers fonne,
Bafe borne, and bafe begot, no *Fauconbridge*.

Indeede the world reputes him lawfull heire,
My father in his life did count him so,
And here my mother stands to proue him so :
But I (my Lord) can proue, and doe auerre
Both to my mothers shame, and his reproach,
He is no heire, nor yet legitimate.
Then (gratious Lord) let *Fauconbridge* enjoy
The living that belongs to *Fauconbridge.*
And let not him possesse anothers right.

 K. Iohn. Proue this, the land is thine by *Englands* lawe.

 Q. Elian. Vngratious youth, to rip thy mothers shame,
The wombe from whence thou didst thy being take,
All honest eares abhorre thy wickednesse,
But Gold I see doth beate downe Natures lawe.

 Mother. My gratious Lord, and you thrice reuerend
That see the teares distilling from mine eies, (Dame,
And scalding sighes blowne from a rented heart:
For honour and regard of womanhood,
Let me intreate to be commaunded hence.
Let not these eares heere receiue the hissing sound,
Of such a viper, who with poysoned words
Doth masserate the bowels of my soule.

 K. Iohn. Lady, stand up, be patient for awhile:
And fellow, say, whose bastard is thy brother ?

 Philip. Not for my selfe, nor for my mother now :
But for the honour of so braue a man,
Whom hee accuseth with adulterie :
Heere I beseech your Grace vpon my knees,
To count him mad, and so dismisse vs hence.

 Robert. Nor mad, nor mazde, but well aduised, I
Charge thee before this royall presence here
To be a bastard to King *Richards* selfe.

Sonne

Sonne to your Grace, and brother to your Maieſtie.
Thus bluntly, and————

  Q. Elian. Yong man, thou needſt not be aſhamed of thy
Nor of thy Sire. But forward with thy proofe. '(kin,

  Robert. The proofe ſo plain, the argument ſo ſtrong,
As that your Highneſſe and theſe noble Lords,
And all (ſaue thoſe that haue no eies to ſee)
Shall ſweare him to be baſtard to the King.
Firſt, when my Father was Embaſſador
In *Germanie* vnto the Emperour,
The King lay often at my fathers houſe;
And all the realme ſuſpeated what befell:
And at my fathers back-returne agen
My mother was deliuered, as tis ſed,
Sixe weeks before the account my father made.
But more than this: looke but on *Philips* face,
His features, actions, and his lineaments,
And all this princely preſence ſhall confeſſe,
He is no other but King *Richards* ſonne.
Then gratious Lord, reſt he King *Richards* ſonne,
And let me reſt ſafe in my Fathers right,
That am his rightfull ſonne and only heire.

  K. Iohn. Is this thy proofe, and all thou haſt to ſay?
  Robert: I haue no more, nor neede I greater proofe.

  K. Iohn. Firſt, where thou ſaidſt in abſence of thy Sire
My brother often lodged in his houſe:
And what of that? baſe groome to ſlaunder him,
That honoured his Embaſſador ſo much,
In abſence of the man to cheere the wife?
This will not hold, proceede vnto the next.

  Q. Elian. Thou ſaiſt ſhe teemde ſixe weekes before her
Why good ſir Squire, are you ſo cunning growen, (time

                                  To

To make account of womens reckonings?
Spit in your hand and to your other proofes:
Many mischances happen in such affaires,
To make a woman come before her time.

  K. Iohn. And where thou saist, he looketh like the King,
In action, feature and proportion:
Therein I hold with thee, for in my life
I neuer saw so liuely counterfet
Of *Richard Cordelion,* as in him.

  Robert. Then good my Lord, be you indifferent Iudge,
And let me haue my lining and my right.

  Q. Elianor. Nay, heare you sir, you runne away too fast:
Know you not, *Omne simile non est idem?*
Or haue read in. Hark yee, good sir,
Twas thus I warrant, and no otherwise,
Shee lay with sir *Robert* your father, and thought vpon
King *Richard* my sonne, and so your brother was formed
in this fashion.

  Robert. Madame, you wrong me thus to iest it out,
I craue my right, King *Iohn,* as thou art King,
So be thou iust, and let me haue my right.

  K. Iohn. Why (foolish boy) thy proofes are friuolous,
Nor canst thou challenge any thing thereby.
But thou shalt see how I will helpe thy claime:
This is my doome, and this my doome shall stand
Irreuocable, as I am King of *England.*
For thou know'st not, weele aske of them that know,
His mother and himselfe shall end this strife:
And as they say, so shall thy liuing passe.

  Robert. My Lord, herein I challenge you of wrong,
To giue away my right, and put the doome
Vnto themselues. Can there be likelihood

                    That.

That fhee will loofe?
Or he will giue the liuing from himfelfe ?
It may not be, my Lord. Why fhould it be ?

K. Iohn. Lords, keep him back, and let him heare the
doom. *Effex*, firft afk the mother thrice, who was his Sire?

Effex. Lady *Margaret,* widow of *Fauconbridge,*
Who was Father to thy Sonne *Philip ?*

Mother. Pleafe it your Maiefty, Sir *Rob. Fauconbridge.*
Rob. This is right, afke my fellow there if I be a thiefe.
K. Iohn. Afke *Philip* whofe fonne he is.
Effex. Philip, who was thy father?

Philip. Mas my Lord, and that's a queftion : and you
had not taken fome paines with her before, I fhould
have defired you to afke my mother.

K. Iohn. Say, who was thy Father ?
Philip. Faith (my Lord) to anfwere you, fure hee is
my father that was neereft my mother when I was begotten, and him I think to be Sir *Robert Fauconbridge.*

K. Iohn. Effex, for fafhions fake demand agen,
And fo an end to this contention.

Robert. Was ever man thus wronged as *Robert* is ?
Effex. Philip fpeake I fay, who was thy father ?
K. Iohn. Young man how now, what art thou in a trance?
Q. Elianor. Philip awake, the man is in a dreame.
Philip. Philippus atauis edite Regibus.
What faift thou *Philip,* fprung of auncient Kings ?
————*Quo me rapit tempeftas ?*
What winde of honour blowes this furie forth ?
Or whence proceede thefe fumes of Maieftie ?
Methinkes I hear a hollow Ecchoe found,
That *Philip* is the fonne vnto a King:
The whiftling leaues vpon the trembling trees,

Whiftle

Whistle in confort I am *Richards* sonne:
The bubling murmur of the waters fall
Records *Philippus Regius filius :*
Birds in their flight make muficke with their wings,
Filling the aire with glorie of my birth :
Birds, bubbles, leaues, and mountaines, Ecchoe, all
Ring in mine eares, that I am *Richards* sonne.
Fond man! ah whither art thou carried ?
How are thy thoughts ywrapt in Honors heauen ?
Forgetfull what thou art, and whence thou camft.
Thy Fathers land cannot maintain thefe thoughts;
Thefe thoughts are farre vnfitting *Fauconbridge :*
And well they may; for why this mounting minde
Doth foare too high to ftoupe to *Fauconbridge.*
Why how now ? knoweft thou where thou art ?
And knoweft thou who expects thine anfwer here ?
Wilt thou vpon a frantick-madding vaine
Goe loofe thy land, and fay thy felfe bafe borne?
No, keep thy land, though *Richard* were thy Sire.
What ere thou thinkft, fay thou art *Fauconbridge.*

    K. Iohn. Speake man, be fodaine, who thy Father was.
    Philip. Pleafe it your Maieftie, Sir *Robert.*
Philip, that *Fauconbridge* cleaues to thy iawes:
It will not out, I cannot for my life
Say I am fonne vnto a *Fauconbridge.*
Let land and liuing goe, tis Honors fire
That makes me fweare King *Richard* was my Sire:
Bafe to a King addes title of more State,
Than Knights begotten; though legitimate
Pleafe it your Grace, I am King *Richards* Sonne.

                                    Robert.

Robert. Robert reuiue thy heart, let forrow die,
His faltring tongue not fuffers him to lie.

Mo. What head-ftrong furie doth enchant my fonne?
Philip, Philip cannot repent, for he hath done.

K. Iohn. Then *Philip* blame not me, thy felfe haft loft
By wilfullneffe, thy liuing and thy land.
Robert, thou art the heire of *Fauconbridge,*
God giue thee ioy, greater than thy defert.

Q. Elian. Why how now *Philip,* giue away thine own?

Philip. Madame, I am bold to make myfelfe your
The pooreft kinfman that your Highneffe hath: (nephew,
And with this Prouerb gin the world anew;
Help hands, I haue no lands, Honor is my defire;
Let *Philip* liue to fhew himfelfe worthy fo great a Sire.

Q. Elian. Phil. I think thou knewft thy Grandams minde;
But cheere thee Boy, I will not fee thee want
As long as *Elianor* hath foote of land:
Hencefoorth thou fhalt be taken for my fonne,
And waite on me and on thine vncle heere,
Who fhall giue honour to thy noble mind.

K. Iohn. Philip kneele down, that thou maift throughly
How much thy refolution pleafeth vs, (know
Rife up Sir *Richard Plantaginet* King *Richards* Sonne.

Philip. Grant heauens that *Philip* once may fhew him-
Worthy the honour of *Plantaginet,* (felfe
Or bafeft glorie of a Baftards name.

K. Iohn. Now, Gentlemen, we will away to *Fraunce,*
To checke the pride of *Arthur* and his mates:
Effex, thou fhalt be Ruler of my Realme,
And toward the maine charges of my warres,
Ile ceaze the lafie Abbey lubbers lands
Into my hands to pay my men of warre.

The

The Pope and Popelings shall not grease themselues
With gold and groates, that are the souldiers due.
Thus forward Lords, let our commaund be done,
And march we forward mightily to *Fraunce*.   [*Exeunt*.

Manent Philip *and his Mother*.

Philip. Madame, I beseech you deigne me so much
leasure as the hearing of a matter that I long to impart
to you.

Mother. What's the matter *Philip?* I think your suit
in secret, tends to some money matter, which you sup-
pose burns in the bottom of my chest.

Philip. No Madame, it is no such suit as to beg or bor-
But such a suit, as might some other grant,   (row
I would not now have troubled you withall.

Mother. A Gods name let vs heare it.

Philip. Then Madame thus, your Ladiship sees well,
How that my scandal growes by meanes of you,
In that report hath rumord vp and downe,
I am a bastard, and no *Fauconbridge*.
This grosse attaint so tilteth in my thoughts,
Maintaining combat to abridge mine ease,
That field and towne, and company alone,
What so I do, or wheresoere I am,
I cannot chase the slaunder from my thoughts.
If it be true, resolue me of my sire,
For pardon, Madame, if I think amisse.
Be *Philip Philip*, and no *Fauconbridge*,
His father doubtlesse was as braue a man.
To you on knees, as sometime *Phaeton*,
Mistrusting sielly *Merop* for his sire,

I   Straining

Straining a little bashfull modestie,
I beg some instance whence I am extraught.
  Mother. Yet more adoe to haste me to my graue,
And wilt thou too become a mothers crosse?
Must I accuse my selfe to close with you?
Slaunder my selfe, to quiet your affects?
Thou moust me *Philip* with this idle talke,
Which I remit, in hope this mood will die.
  Philip. Nay, Lady mother, heare me further yet,
For strong conceit drives duty hence awhile :
Your husband, *Fauconbridge,* was father to that sonne,
That carries markes of nature like the fire,
The sonne that blotteth you with wedlockes breach,
And holds my right as lineal in descent
From him whose forme was figured in his face.
Can Nature so dissemble in her frame,
To make the one so like as like may be,
And in the other print no character
To challenge any marke of true descent?
My brothers mind is base, and too too dull,
To mount where *Philip* lodgeth his affects
And his externall graces that you viewe,
(Though I report it) counterpoise not mine :
His constitution plaine debilitie,
Requires the chaire, and mine the seat of steele.
Nay, what is he, or what am I to him?
When any one that knoweth how to carpe,
Will scarcely iudge us both one countrey borne.
This, Madame, this, hath droue me from my selfe :
And here by heauens eternal lampes I sweare,
As cursed *Nero* with his mother did,
So I with you, if you resolue me not.
                    C   *Moth.*

Moth. Let mothers teares quench out thy angers fire,
And vrge no further what thou doeft require.

Phil. Let fonnes intreatie fway the mother now,
Or elfe fhe dies : Ile not infringe my vow.

Moth. Vnhappy tafke : muft I recount my fhame,
Blab my mifdeeds, or by concealing die?
Some power ftrike me fpeechlefs for a time,
Or take from him awhile his hearings ufe.
Why wifh I fo, vnhappy as I am?
The fault is mine, and he the faultie fruit,
I blufh, I faint, oh would I might be mute.

Phil. Mother be briefe, I long to know my name.

Moth. And longing die, to fhroud thy mothers fhame.

Phil. Come Madame, come, you need not be fo loath,
The fhame is fhared equall twixt vs both,
Ift not a flackeneffe in me, worthy blame,
To be fo old, and cannot write my name?
Good mother refolue me.

Moth. Then *Philip* heare thy fortune, and my griefe,
My honours loffe by purchafe of thy felfe,
My fhame, thy name, and hufbands fecret wrong,
All maimd and ftaind by youths vnruly fway.
And when thou know'ft from whence thou art extraught,
Or if thou knew'ft what fuites, what threats, what feares,
To moue by loue, or maffacre by death,
To yeeld with loue, or end by loues contempt
The mightineffe of him that courted me,
Who tempered terror with his wanton talke,
That fomething may extenuate the guilt.
But let it not aduantage me fo much ;
Vpbraid me rather with the Romane dame
That fhed her blood to wafh away her fhame.

                                            Why

Why stand I to expostulate the crime
With *pro & contra*, now the deed is done?
When to conclude two words may tell the tale,
That *Philips* father was a princes sonne :
Rich *Englands* rule, worlds onely terror he,
For honors losse left me with child of thee :
Whose sonne thou art, then pardon me the rather,
For fair King *Richard* was thy noble father.

  Phil. Then *Robin Fauconbridge* I wish thee ioy,
My sire a King, and I a landlesse boy.
Gods lady mother, the world is in my debt,
There's something owing to *Plantaginet*.
I marry sir, let me alone for game,
Ile act some wonders now I know my name.
By blessed *Mary* Ile not sell that pride
For *Englands* wealth, and all the world beside.
Sit fast the proudest of my fathers foes,
Away good mother, there the comfort goes.   [*Exeunt*,

  Enter Philip the French *King, and* Lewis, Limoges,
    Constance, *and her sonne* Arthur.

  K. Phil. Now gin we broach the title of thy claime,
Young *Arthur*, in the Albion territories,
Skaring proud *Angiers* with a puissant siege :
Braue *Austria*, cause of *Cordelions* death,
Is also come to aide thee in thy warres ;
And all our Forces ioyne for *Arthurs* right.
And, but for causes of great consequence,
Pleading delay till newes from *England* come,
Twice should not *Titan* hide him in the West,
To coole the fet-locks of his wearie teame,
Till I had with an vnresisted shocke

Controld

Controld the marinage of prowd *Angiers* walls,
Or made a forfet of my fame to chaunce.

Conſt. May be that *Iohn* in conſcience or in feare
To offer wrong where you impugne the ill,
Will ſend ſuch calme conditions backe to *Fraunce,*
As ſhall rebate the edge of fearefull warres:
If ſo, forbearance is a deed well done.

Arth. Ah mother, poſſeſſion of a Crowne is much,
And *Iohn* as I have heard reported of,
For preſent vantage will aduenture farre.
The world can witneſſe, in his Brothers time,
He took upon him rule, and almoſt raigne:
Then muſt it follow as a doubtfull point,
That hee'l reſigne the rule vnto his Nephew.
I rather thinke the menace of the world,
Sounds in his eares, as threats of no eſteeme,
And ſooner would he ſcorne *Europa's* power,
Then looſe the ſmalleſt title he enjoyes;
For queſtionleſs he is an Engliſhman.

Lewis. Why are the Engliſh peereleſſe in compare?
Braue Caualiers as ere that Iſland bred,
Haue liu'd and di'd, and dar'd, and done enough,
Yet neuer grac'd their countrey for the cauſe:
England is *England*, yeelding good and bad,
And *Iohn* of *England* is as other *Iohns*.
Truſt me young *Arthur*, if thou like my reed,
Praiſe thou the *French* that help thee in this need.

Limog. The *Engliſhman* hath little cauſe I trowe,
To ſpend good ſpeaches on ſo proud a foe,
Why *Arthur* here's his ſpoyle that now is gone,
Who when he liu'd outrou'd his brother *Iohn*:

But

But haftie curres that lie fo long to catch,
Come halting home, and meete their ouor-match.
But news comes now, here's the Embaffador.

Enter Chattillion.

K. *Phil.* And in good time, welcome my Lord *Chattil-*
What newes? will *Iohn* accord to our command? *(lion:*
 Chat. Be I not briefe to tell your highneffe all,
He will approach to interrupt my tale:
For one felfe bottome brought vs both to *Fraunce,*
He on his part will trie the chance of warre,
And if his words inferre affured truth,
Will loofe himfelfe, and all his followers,
Ere yeeld vnto the leaft of your demands.
The mother Queene fhe taketh on amaine
Gainft Lady *Conftance,* counting her the canfe
That doth Effect this claime to *Albion,*
Coniuring *Arthur* with a grindames care,
To leaue his mother; willing him fubmit
His ftate to *Iohn,* and her protection,
Who (as fhe faith) are ftudious for his good.
More circumftance the feafon intercepts;
This is the fumme, which briefly I have fhowne.
 K. *Phil.* This bitter wind muft nip fome-bodies fpring,
Sodaine and briefe, why fo, tis harneft weather.
But fay, *Chattilion,* what perfons of account are with him?
 Chat. Of *England,* Earle *Pembroke* and *Salifburie,*
The onely noted men of any name.
Next them, a baftard of the Kings deceaft,
A hardie wild-head, tough and venturous,
With many other men of high refolue.
C 3   Then

Then is there with them *Elianor* Mother Queene,
And *Blanch* her Neece, daughter to the King of Spaine:
These are the prime birds of this hot adventure.

Enter King Iohn *and his followers, Queene* Eliahor, Philip
the Baſtard, Earles, &c.

K. Phil. Me ſeemeth *Iohn,* an ouer-daring ſpirit
Effects ſome frenſie in thy raſh approach,
Treading my Confines with thy armed troupes.
I rather lookt for ſome ſubmiſſe reply
Touching the claime thy Nephew *Arthur* makes
To that which thou unjuſtly doſt vſurpe.

K. Iohn. For that *Chattilion* can diſcharge you all,
I liſt not pleade my title with my tongue.
Nor came I hither with intent of wrong
To *Fraunci* or thee, or any right of thine;
But in defence and purchaſe of my right,
The towne of *Angiers:* which thou doſt begirt
In the behalfe of Lady *Conſtance* ſonne,
Whereto nor he nor ſhe can lay iuſt claime.

Conſt. Yes (falſe intruder) if that iuſt be iuſt,
And head-ſtrong vſurpation put apart,
Arthur my Sohne, heire to thy elder brother,
Without ambiguous ſhadow of diſcent,
Is Soueraigne to the ſubſtance thou witholdſt.

Q. Elian. Miſgouernd goſſip, ſtaine to this reſort,
Occaſion of theſe vndecided iarres,
I ſay (that know) to checke thy vaine ſuppoſe,
Thy ſonne hath nought to do with that he claimes.
For proofe whereof, I can inferre a Will,
That barres the way he vrgeth by diſcent.

Conſt.

Conſt. A Will indeed, a crabbed womans will,
Wherein the diuell is an ouerſeer,
And proud dame *Elianor* ſole Exeсutreſſe:
More wills than ſo, on perill of my ſoule,
Were neuer made to hinder *Arthurs* right.

Arth. But ſay there was, as ſure there can be none,
The Law intends ſuch teſtaments as void,
Where right diſcent can no way be impeacht.

Q. Elian. Peace *Arthur* peace, thy mother makes thee
To ſoare with perill after *Icarus*,   (wings
And truſt me yongling for the Fathers ſake,
I pity much the hazard of thy youth.

Conſt. Beſhrew you elſe how pittifull you are,
Ready to weepe to hear him aſke his owne;
Sorrow betide ſuch Grandames and ſuch griefe,
That miniſter a Poyſon for pure loue,
But who ſo blind, as cannot ſee this beame,
That you forſooth would keepe your couſin downe,
For feare his mother ſhould be vs'd too well?
I there's the griefe, confuſion catch the braine,
That hammers ſhifts to ſtop a Princes raigne.

Q. Elian. Impatient, franticke, common ſlaunderer,
Immodeſt dame, vnnurtur'd quarreller,
I tell thee I, not enuie to thy ſonne,
But iuſtice makes me ſpeake as I haue done.

K. Phil. But here's no proofe that ſhews your ſon a king:
K. Io. What wants, my ſword ſhal more at large ſet down
Lew. But that may break before the truth be known.
Phil. Then this may hold till all his right be ſhowne.
Lim. Good words ſir ſauce, your betters are in place,
Phil. Not you ſir doughtie, with your Lyons caſe.
                                             Blanch

Blanch. Ah ioy betide his foul, to whom that spoyle
Ah *Richard*, how thy glory here is wrong'd. (belong'd:
  Lim. Me thinks that *Richards* pride and *Richards* fall,
Should be a president t'affright you all.
  Phil. What words are thefe? how do my finews shake?
My fathers foe clad in my fathers spoyle,
A thoufand furies kindle with reuenge
This heart that choller keepes a confiftorie,
Searing my inwards with a brand of hate:
How doth *Alecto* whifper in mine eares,
Delay not *Philip*, kill the villaine ftraight,
Difrobe him of the matchleffe monument
Thy fathers triumph ore the Sauages?
Bafe heardgroom, coward, peafant, worfe than a threfhing
What mak'ft thou with the Trophie of a King?   (flaue
Sham'ft thou not coyftrell, loathfome dunghill fwad,
To grace thy carkaffe with an ornament
Too pretious for a Monarkes couerture?
Scarce can I temper due obedience
Vnto the prefence of my Soueraigne,
From acting outrage on this trunk of hate:
But arme thee traytor, wronger of renowne,
For by his foule I fweare, my fathers foule,
Twife will I not reuiew the mornings rife,
Till I haue torne that trophie from thy backe,
And fplit thy heart for wearing it fo long.
Philip hath fworne, and if it be not done,
Let not the world repute me *Richards* fonne.
  Lim. Nay foft fir baftard, hearts are not fplit fo foone,
Let them reioyce that at the end doe win:
And take this leffon at thy foe-mans hand,
Pawne not thy life to get thy Fathers fkin.

                                        Blanch.

Blanch. Wel may the world ſpeake of his knightly valor,
That wins this hide to weare a Ladies fauour.

Phil. Ill may I thriue, and nothing brooke with me,
If ſhortly I preſent it not to thee.

K. Phil. Lordings forbeare, for time is comming faſt,
That deeds may trie what words can not determine,
And to the purpoſe for the cauſe you come.
Me ſeemes you ſet right in chaunce of warre,
Yeelding no other reaſons for your claime,
But ſo and ſo, becauſe it ſhall be ſo.
So wrong ſhall be ſubornd by truſt of ſtrength :
A tyrants practiſe to inueſt himſelfe,
Where weake reſiſtance giueth wrong the way.
To checke the which, in holy lawfull armes,
I, in the right of *Arthur*, *Geffreys* ſonne,
Am come before this city of *Angiers*,
To barre all other falſe ſuppoſed claime,
From whence, or howſoere the error ſprings.
And in his quarrel on my princely word,
Ile fight it out vnto the lateſt man.

K. Iohn. Know King of *Fraunce*, I will not be com-
By any power or prince in Chriſtendome,   (manded
To yeelde an inſtance how I hold mine owne,
More than to anſwere, that mine owne is mine,
But wilt thou ſee me parley with the towne,
And heare them offer me allegeance,
Fealtie and homage, as true liege men ought ?

K. Phil. Summon them, I will not beleeue it till I ſee it.
and when I ſee it, Ile ſoone change it.

Tho

They summon the Towne, the Citizens appeare upon the walls.

K. Iohn. You men of *Angiers*, and as I take it my loiall
subiects, I haue summoned you to the walls: to dispute on
my right, were to thinke you doubtfull therein, which I
am perswaded you are not. In few words, our brothers
sonne, backt with the king of *Fraunce*, haue beleagred
your towne vpon a false pretended title to the same: in
defence whereof I your liege Lord haue brought our power
to fence you from the Vsurper, to free your intended ser-
uitude, and utterly to supplant the foemen, to my right
and your rest. Say then, who keep you the town for?

Citiz. For our lawfull King.

K. Iohn. I was no less perswaded: then in Gods name
open your gates, and let me enter.

Citiz. And it please your Highnes we comptroll not
your title, neither will we rashly admit your entrance: if
you be lawfull King, with all obedience we keep it to
your use, if not King, our rashnes to be impeached for
yielding, without more considerate triall; wee answer
not as men lawlesse, but to the behoofe of him that
prooues lawfull,

K. Iohn. I shall not come in then?

Citiz. No my Lord, till we know more.

K. Phil. Then heare me speak in the behalfe of *Arthur*
sonne of *Gaffrey*, elder brother to *Iohn*, his title manifest,
without contradiction, to the crowne and kingdom of
England, with *Angiers*, and diuers townes on this side
the sea: wil you acknowledge him your liege Lord,
who speaketh in my word, to entertain you with all fauours, as beseemeth a King to his subiects, or a friend

to

to his wellwillers; or ftand to the peril of your contempt,
when his title is proued by the fword.

Citiz. We anfwer as before, till you haue proued one
right, we acknowledge none right; he that tries himfelfe our Soueraigne, to him wil we remaine firme fubiects, and for him, and in his right we hold our towne,
as defirous to know the truth, as loth to fubfcribe before
we know: more than this we cannot fay, and more than
this we dare not do.

K. Phil. Then *Iohn* I defy thee, in the name and behalfe of *Arthur Plantaginet*, thy king and coufin; whofe
right and patrimony thou detaineft; as I doubt not, ere
the day end, in a fet-battle make thee confeffe; where-
unto, with a zeal to right, I challenge thee.

K. Iohn. I accept thy challenge, and turne the defiance
to thy throat.

Excurfions. The Baftard chafeth Limoges *the Auftrich
Duke, and maketh him leaue the Lyons fkin.*

Phil. And art thou gone misfortune haunt thy fteps,
And chill cold feare affaile thy times of reft.
Morpheus leaue here thy filent Eban caue,
Befiege his thoughts with difmal fantafies,
And ghaftly obiects of pale threatning *Mars.*
Affright him euery minute with ftearne lookes,
Let fhadow temper terror in his thoughts,
And let the terror make the coward mad,
And in his madneffe let him feare purfuit,
And fo in frenfie let the peafant die.
Here is the ranfome that allaies his rage,
The firft freehold that *Richard* left his fonne:

With

With which I fhall furprize his liuing foes,
As *Hectors* ftatue did the fainting *Greekes.*   [*Exit.*

*Enter the Kings Herolds with Trumpets to the wals of
Angiers: they fummon the Towne.*

Eng. Her. *Iohn* by the grace of God King of England,
Lord of Ireland, Aniou, Toraine, &c. demandeth once
again of you his fubiects of Angiers, if you wil quietly
furrender up the towne into his hands?
Fr. Her. *Philip* by the grace of God King of *Fraunce,*
demaundeth in the behalfe of *Arthur* Duke of *Britaine,*
if you will furrender vp the towne into his hands, to the
vfe of the faid *Arthur.*
Citizens. Herolds go tell the two victorious Princes,
that we the poor Inhabitants of *Angiers,* require a parley of their Maiefties.
Herolds. We goe.

Enter the Kings, *Queene* Elianor, Blanch, Philip *the Baftard,* Limoges, Lewis, Chattilion, Pembroke, Salifbury, Conftance, *and* Arthur.

K. Iohn. Herold, what anfwer do the Townfmen fend?
Philip. Will *Angiers* yeeld to *Philip* King of *Fraunce?*
Eng. Her. The townfmen on the wals accept your Grace.
Fr. Her. And craue a parley of your Maiefty.
K. Iohn. You citizens of *Angiers,* haue your eyes
Beheld the flaughter that our *Englifh* bowes
Haue made vpon the coward fraudfull *French?*
And haue you wifely pondred therewithall
Your gaine in yeelding to the *Englifh* King?

Lewis

K. Phil. Their loffe in yeelding to the *Englifh* King.
But *Iohn,* they faw from out their higheft towers
The Chenaliers of *Fraunce* and croffe-bow-fhot
Make lanes of flaughtered bodies through thine hoaft,
And are refolu'd to yeeld to *Arthurs* right.   (wals,

K. Iohn. Why *Philip,* though thou brauft it fore the
Thy confcience knowes that *Iohn* hath wonne the field.

K. Phil. What ere my confcience knowes, thy army
That *Philip* had the better of the day.   [feeles

Phil. *Philip* indeed had got the Lions cafe,
Which here he holds to *Limoges* difgrace.
Bafe Duke to flie and leaue fuch fpoiles behind:
But this thou knewft of force to make me ftay.
It farde with thee as with the mariner,
Spying the hugie Whale, whofe monftrous bulke
Doth beare the waues like mountaines fore the wind,
That throws out emptie ueffels, fo to ftay
His fury, while the fhip doth fayle away.
Philip 'tis thine: and fore this princely prefence,
Madame, I humbly lay it at your feete,
Being the firft aduenture I atchieu'd,
And firft exploite your Grace did me enioyne:
Yet many more I long to be enioyn'd.

Blanch. *Philip* I take it, and I thee command
To weare the fame as earft thy father did:
Therewith receiue this fauour at my hands,
T'incourage thee to follow *Richards* fame.

Arth. Ye Citizens of *Angiers* are ye mute?
Arthur or *Iohn,* fay which fhall be your King?

Citizen. We care not which, if once we knew the right:
But till we know, we will not yeeld our right.

Phil. Might *Philip* counfell two fo mightie Kings,

D   As

As are the Kings of *England* and of *Fraunce*,
He would aduise your Graces to vnite
And knit your forces gainst thefe citizens,
Pulling their battred wals about their eares.
The towne once wonne, then striue about the claime,
For they are minded to delude you both.

  Citiz. Kings, Princes, Lords and Knights assembled
The Citizens of *Angiers* all by me   (here,
Entreate your Maiestie to heare them speake :
And as you like the motion they shall make,
So to account and follow their aduice.

  K. Iohn. K. Phil. Speake on, we giue thee leaue.

  Citiz. Then thus : whereas the young and lusty knight
Incites you on to knit your kingly strengths :
The motion cannot chuse but please the good,
And such as loue the quiet of the State.
But how my Lords, how shold your strengths be knit?
Not to oppresse your subiects and your friends,
And fill the world with brawles and mutinies,
But vnto peace your forces should be knit
To liue in Princely league and amitie :
Doe this, the gates of *Angiers* shall giue way,
And stand wide open to your hearts content.
To make this peace a lasting bond of loue,
Remains one onely honourable meanes,
Which by your pardon I shall here display.
Lewis the Dolphin and the heire of *Fraunce*,
A man of noted valour through the world,
Is yet vnmarried : let him take to wife
The beauteous daughter of the King of *Spaine*,
Neece to K. *Iohn*, the louely Lady *Blanch*,
Begotten on his sister *Elianor*,

With

With her in marriage will her vnkle giué
Caftles and towers, as fitteth fuch a match.
The Kings thus ioynd in league of perfect loue,
They may fo deale with *Arthur* Duke of *Britaine.*
Who is but young, and yet vnmeet to raigne,
As he fhall ftand contented euery way.
Thus haue I boldly (for the common good)
Deliuered what the Citie gaue in charge.
And as upon conditions you agree,
So fhall we ftand content to yeeld the towne.

   Arth. A proper peace; if fuch a motion hold;
Thefe Kings beare armes for me, and for my right,
And they fhall fhare my lands to make them friends.

   Q. Elian. Sonne *Iohn,* follow this motion, as thou lo-
ueft thy mother.
Make league with *Philip,* yeeld to any thing:
Lewis fhall haue my neece, and then be fure
Arthur fhall haue fmall fuccour out of *Fraunce.*

   K. Iohn. Brother of *Fraunce,* you heare the Citizens:
Then tell me, how you meane to deale herein.

   Conft. Why *Iohn,* what canft thou giue unto thy neece,
That haft no foote of land, but *Arthurs* right?

   Lew. Birlady Citizens, I like your choyce,
A louely damfell is the lady *Blanch,*
Worthy the heire of *Europe* for her pheere.

   Conft. What Kings, why ftand you gazing in a trance?
Why how now Lords? accurfed Citizens
To fill and tickle their ambitious eares,
With hope of gaine, that fprings from *Arthurs* loffe;
Some difmall Planet at thy birth-day raign'd,
For now I fee the fall of all thy hopes.

K. Phil.

K. Phil. Ladie, and Duke of *Britaine*, know you both,
The king of *Fraunce* refpects his honor more,
Than to betray his friends and fauourers.
Princeffe of *Spaine*, could you affect my Sonne,
If we upon conditions could agree ?

Phil. Swounds Madam, take an *Englifh* Gentleman ?
Slaue as I was, I thought to have mou'd the match.
Grandame you made me halfe a promife once,
That ladie *Blanch* fhould bring me wealth inough,
And make me heire of ftore of *Englifh* land.

Q. Elian. Peace *Philip*, I will looke thee out a wife,
We muft with policie compound this ftrife.

Phil. If *Lewis* get her, well, I fay no more :
But let the frollicke *Frenchman* take no fcorne,
If *Philip* front him with an *Englifh* horne.

K. Iohn. Ladie, what anfwer make you to the King of
Can you affect the Dolphin for your Lord ?   *(Fraunce?*

Blanch. I thank the King that likes of me fo well,
To make me Bride unto fo great a Prince :
But giue me leaue my Lord to paufe on this,
Leaft being too too forward in the caufe,
It may be blemifh to my modeftie.

Q. Elian. Sonne *Iohn*, and worthy *Philip* K. of *Fraunce*,
Do you confer awhile about the Dower,
And I will fchoole my Modeft Neece fo well,
That fhe fhall yeeld as foon as you haue done.

Conftance. I, there's the wretch that brocheth all this il,
Why flie I not vpon the Beldams face,
And with my nayles pull forth her hatefull eyes ?

Arthur. Sweet mother ceafe thefe haftie madding fits :
For my fake, let my Grandame haue her will.
O would fhe with her hands pull forth my heart,
I could afford it to appeafe thefe broyles.   But

But (mother) let vs wifely wink at all,
Leaft farther harmes enfue our haftie fpeech.

   K. Phil. Brother of *England,* what dowrie wilt thou giue
Vnto my fonne in marriage with thy neece ?

   K. Iohn. Firft *Philip* knows her dowrie out of *Spaine,*
To be fo great as may content a King :
But more to mend and amplifie the fame,
I giue in money thirtie thoufand markes.
For land I leaue it to thine owne demand.

   K. Phil. Then I demand *Volqueffon, Torain, Main,*
Poitiers and *Aniou,* thefe fiue Prouinces,
Which thou as King of *England* holdft in *Fraunce :*
Then fhall our peace be foone concluded on.

   Phil. No leffe then fiue fuch Prouinces at once ?

   K. Iohn. Mother what fhall I do ? my brother got thefe
With much effufion of our *Englifh* bloud :   (lands
And fhall I giue it all away at once ?

   Q. Elian. Iohn giue it him, fo fhalt thou liue in peace,
And keep the refidue fans ieopardie.

   K. Iohn. Philip, bring forth thy fonne, here is my neece,
And here in marriage I do giue with her
From me and my fucceffors, *Englifh* Kings,
Volqueffon, Poiters, Aniou, Torain, Main,
And thirtie thoufand markes of ftipend coyne:
Now citizens, how like you of this match ?

   Citiz. We ioy to fee fo fweete a peace begun.

   Lewis. Lewis with *Blanch* fhall euer liue content.
But now King *Iohn,* what fay you to the Duke ?
Father, fpeake as you may in his behalfe.

   K. Phil. K. Iohn, be good vnto thy nephew here,
And giue him fomewhat that fhall pleafe you beft.

K. Iohn. Arthur, although thou troubleſt *Englands*
Yet hereI giue thee *Britaine* for thine owne,   (peace,
Together with the Earledome of *Richmont,*
And this rich citie of *Angiers* withall.

 Q. Elian. And if thou ſeeke to pleaſe thine Vncle *Iohn*
Shalt ſee my ſonne how I will make of thee.

K. Iohn. Now euery thing is ſorted to this end,
Lets in, and there prepare the marriage rites.
Which in St. *Maries* Chappel preſently
Shall be performed ere this preſence part.   [*Exeunt.*

         Manent Conſtance *and* Arthur.

Arth. Madame good cheére, theſe drouping languiſh-
Add no redreſs to ſalue our awkward haps,.   (ments
If heauens haue concluded theſe euents,,
To ſmall auaile is bitter penſiueneſs :
Seaſons will change, and ſo our preſent greeſe
May change with them, and all to our releeſe.

Conſt. Ah boy, thy eares I ſee are farre too greene
To looke into the bottome of theſe cares.
But I, who ſee the poyſe that weigheth downe
Thy weale, my wiſh, and all the willing meanes
Wherewith thy fortune and thy fame ſhould mount—
What ioy, what eaſe, what reſt can lodge in me,
With whom all hope and hap do diſagree ?

Arth. Yet ladies teares, and cares, and ſolemn ſhewes,
Rather than helpes, heape vp more worke for woes.

Conſt. If any power will heare a widowes plaint,
That from a wounded ſoule implores reuenge ;
Send fell contagion to infect this clime,
This curſed countrey, where the traitors breath,
Whoſe periurie (as proud *Briareus,)*
Beleaguers all the ſkie with miſ-beleeſe.

                                        He

He promift *Arthur*, and he fware it too,
To fence thy right, aud check thy fo-mans pride :
But now black-fpotted periurie as he is,
He takes a truce with *Elianors* damned brat,
And marries *Lewis* to her louely neece,
Sharing thy fortune, and thy birth-dayes gift
Between thefe louers : ill betide the match.
And as they fhoulder thee from out thine owne,
And triumph in a widowes tearefull cares :
So heauens croffe them with a thriftlefs courfe.
Is all the bloud yfpilt on either party,
Clofing the cranies of the thirftie earth,
Growne to a loue-game and a bridall feaft ?
And muft thy birth-right bid the wedding banes ?
Poore helpleffe boy, hopeleffe and helpleffe too,
To whom misfortune feems no yoake at all,
Thy ftay, thy ftate, thy imminent mifhaps
Woundeth thy mothers thoughts with feeling care,
Why lookft thou pale ? the colour flies thy face :
I trouble now the fountaine of thy youth,
And make it muddie with my doles difcourfe,
Goe in with me, reply not louely boy,
We muft obfcure this mone with melodie,
Leaft worfer wrack enfue our male-content,   [*Exeunt*.

Enter the King of England, *the King of* France, Arthur,
    Phil. *the* Baftard, Lewis, Limoges, Conftance, Blanch,
    Chattilion, Pembroke, Salifburie, *and* Elianor,

K. Iohn. This is the day, the long-defired day,
Wherein the Realmes of *England* and of *Fraunce*
Stand highly bleffed in a lafting peace.
Thrice happy is the Bridegroome and the Bride,
                                        Krom.

From whose sweet bridall such a concord springs,
To make of mortall foes immortal friends.

　Conft. Vngodly peace made by anothers warre.

　Phil. Vnhappie peace, that ties thee from reuenge,
Rouze thee *Plantaginet*, liue not to see
The Butcher of the great *Plantaginet*.
Kings, Princes, and ye Peers of either realmes,
Pardon my rashnes, and forgiue the zeale
That carries me in furie to a deede
Of high defert, of honour, and of armes.
A boone, (O Kings) a boone doth *Philip* begge
Proftrate upon his knee: which knee shall cleaue
Vnto the fuperficies of the earth,
Till *Fraunce* and *England* grant this glorious boone.

　K. Iohn. Speake *Philip, England* grants thee thy requeft.

　K. Phil. And France confirms what ere is in his Power.

　Phil. Then Duke: fit faft, I leuell at thy head,
Too bafe a ranfome for my fathers life.
Princes I craue the combate with the Duke
That braues it in dishonour of my fire.
Your words are paft, nor can you now reuerfe,
The princely promife that reuiues my foul,
Whereat me thinkes I fee his finews fhake:
This is the boone (dread Lords), which granted once
Or life or death are pleafant to my foule;
Since I fhall liue and die in *Richards* right.

　Lim. Bafe baftard, mifbegotten of a King,
To interrupt thefe holy nuptiall rites
With brawles and tumults to a Dukes difgrace;
Let it fuffice, I fcorne to ioyne in fight,
With one fo fare vnequall to my felfe.

　Phil. A fine excufe, Kings if you will be Kings,
Then keepe your words, and let us combate it.

　　　　　　　　　　　　　　　K. Iohn.

K. Iohn. Philip, we cannot force the Duke to fight,
Beeing a subiect vnto neither realme :
But tell me *Austria,* if an *English* Duke
Should dare thee thus, wouldst thou accept the challenge?

Lim. Else let the world account the *Austrich* Duke
The greatest coward liuing on the earth.

K. Iohn. Then cheere thee *Philip, Iohn* will keep his
Kneele downe, in sight of *Philip* King of *Fraunce,* (word,
And all these princely lords assembled here,
I gird thee with the sword of *Normandie,*
And of that land I do inuest thee Duke :
So shalt thou be in liuing and in land
Nothing inferiour vnto *Austria.*

Lim. K. Iohn, I tell thee flatly to thy face,
Thou wrong'st mine houour : and that thou mai'st see
How much I scorne thy new made Duke and thee,
I flatly say, I will not be compeld :
And so farewel sir Duke of low degree,
Ile find a time to match you for this geare.   [*Exit.*

K. Iohn. Stay *Philip,* let him goe, the honours thine.

Phil. I cannot liue vnless his life be mine.

Q. Elian. Thy forwardnes this day hath ioy'd my soule,
And made me think my *Richard* liues in thee.

K. Phil. Lordings let's in, and spend the wedding day
In maskes and triumphs, letting quarrels cease.

Enter a Cardinal from Rome.

Pand. Stay King of *Fraunce,* I charge thee ioyn not
With him that stands accurst of God and men.   (hands
Know *Iohn,* that I *Pandulph* Cardinall of *Millaine,* and
Legate from the See of *Rome,* demand of thee in the name
of our holy father the Pope *Innocent,* why thou dost (con-
trary

trary to the lawes of our holy mother the church, and our
holy father the Pope) difturb the quiet of the church, and
difanull the election of *Stephen Langhton*, whom his holinesse hath elected Archbishop of *Canterburie*: this in his
holinesse name I demand of thee?

K. Iohn. And what haft thou or the Pope thy mafter to
do to demand of me, how I imploy mine own? Know fir
prieft, as I honor the church and holy church-men, fo I
fcorn to be fubiect to the greateft prelate in the world.
Tell thy mafter fo from me, and fay, *Iohn* of *England*
faid it, that heuer an *Italian* prieft of them all, fhall either
haue tythe, tole, or polling penny out of *England*; but as
I am King, fo will I raigne next under God, fupreame
head both ouer fpiritual and temporall: and he that con-
tradicts me in this, Ile make him hop headlesse.

K. Phil. What *K. Iohn*, know what you fay, thus to
blafpheme againft our holy father the Pope?

K. Iohn. Philip, though thou and all the Princes of Chriftendome fuffer themfelues to be abus'd by a prelates flauery, my mind is not of fuch bafe temper. If the Pope
will be King of *England*, let him win it with the fword, I
know no other title he can alleadge to mine inheritance.

Pand. Iohn, this is thine anfwer?

K. Iohn. What then?

Pand. Then I *Pandulph* of *Padua*, Legate from the
Apoftolike See, do in the name of Saint *Peter* and his
fucceffor our holy father Pope *Innocent*, pronounce thee
accurfed, difcharging euery of thy fubiects of all dutie
and fealtie that they do owe to thee, and pardon and for-
giuenesse of finne to thofe or them whatfoeuer, which fhall
carrie armes againft thee, or murder thee: This I pronounce and charge all good men to abhorre thee as an
excommunicate perfon.

K. Iohn.

K. Iohn. So fir, the more the foxe is curs'd the better
a fares, if God bleſſe me and my land, let the Pope and
his ſhauelings curſe and ſpare not.

Pand. Furthermore, I charge thee *Philip* K. of *Fraunce,*
and all the kings and princes of Chriſtendome, to make
warre upon this miſcreant: and whereas thou haſt made a
league with him, and confirmed it by oath, I do in the
name of our foreſaid father the Pope, acquit thee of that
oath, as vnlawfull, being made with an heretick; howe
ſai'ſt thou *Philip,* do'ſt thou obey?

K. Iohn. Brother of *Fraunce,* what ſay you to the
Cardinall?

K. Phil. I ſay, I am ſorry for your Maieſtie, requeſt-
ing you to ſubmit yourſelfe to the church of *Rome.*

K. Iohn. And what ſay you to our league, if I do not
ſubmit?

K. Phil. What ſhould I ſay? I muſt obey the Pope.

K. Iohn. Obey the Pope, and breake your oath to God?

K. Phil. The Legate hath abſolu'd me of mine oath:
Then yeelde to *Rome,* or I defie thee here.

K. Iohn. Why *Philip,* I defie the Pope and thee,
Falſe as thou art, and periur'd King of *Fraunce,*
Vnworthy man to be accounted King.
Giu'ſt thou thy ſword into a prelates hands?
Pandulph, where I of Abbots, Monkes and Friers
Haue taken ſomewhat to maintaine my wars,
Now will I take no more but all they haue.
Ile rouze the lazy lubers from their cels,
And in deſpite Ile ſend them to the Pope.
Mother come you with me, and for the reſt
That will not follow *Iohn* in this attempt,
Confuſion light upon their damned ſoules.
Come Lords, fight for your K. that fighteth for your good.
                                                    Phil.

K. Phil. And are they gone? thy selfe shalt see
How *Fraunce* will fight for *Rome* and romish rites.
Nobles to armes, let him not passe the seas,
Let's take him captiue, and in triumph lead
The King of *England* to the gates of *Rome.*
Arthur bestirre thee man, and thou shalt see
What *Philip* King of *Fraunce* will do for thee.

Blanch. And will your Grace upon your wedding day
Forsake your bride, and follow dreadfull drums?
Nay, good my Lord, stay you at home with me.

Lew. Sweetheart content thee, and wee shall agree.

K. Phil. Follow my Lords, Lord Cardinall lead the way,
Drums shal be musicke to this wedding day.   [*Exeunt.*

Excursions. Philip *the Bastard pursues* Austria, *and kils him.*

Phil. Thus hath K. *Richards* son performed his vowes,
And offred *Austria's* blood for sacrifice
Vnto his fathers euerliuing soule.
Braue *Cordelion,* now my heart doth say,
I haue deseru'd, though not to be thine heire,
Yet as I am, thy base begotten sonne,
A name as pleasing to thy *Philips* heart,
As to be cald the Duke of *Normandie.*
Lie there a prey to euery rau'ning fowle :
And as my father triumpht in thy spoyles,
And trode thine ensignes underneath his feet,
So do I tread upon thy cursed selfe,
And leaue thy body to the fowles for food.   [*Exit.*

Excursions. Arthur, Constance, Lewis, *hauing taken Queen*
Elianor *Prisoner.*

Const. Thus hath the God of Kings with conquering
Dispearst the foes to true succession,   (arme

                                                    Proud,

Proud, and difturber of thy countries peace,
Conftance doth liue to tame thine infolence,
And on thy head will now auenged be
For all the mifchiefs hatched in thy braine.

   Q. Elian. Contemptuous Dame, unreuerent dutches
      thou,
To braue fo great a Queene as *Elianor*,
Bafe fcold, haft thou forgot, that I was wife
And mother to three mightie *Englifh* Kings?
I charge thee then, and you forfooth fir boy,
To fet your Grandmother at libertie.
And yeeld to *Iohn* your Vncle and your King.

   Conft. 'Tis not thy words proud Queene fhall carry it.

   Elian. Nor yet thy threates, proud Dame, fhall daunt
     my mind.

   Arth. Sweete Grandame, and good mother leaue thefe
     braules.

   Elian. Ile find a time to triumph in thy fall.

   Conft. My time is now to triumph in thy fall,
And thou fhalt know that *Conftance* will triumph.

   Arth. Good mother, weigh it is Queene *Elianor*,
Though fhe be captiue, ufe her like her felfe.
Sweet Grandame beare with what my mother fayes,
Your Highneffe fhall be ufed honourably.

            Enter a Meffenger.

   Meff. *Lewis* my Lord, Duke *Arthur*, and the reft,
To armes in haft, K. *Iohn* relyes his men,
And ginnes the fight afrefh: and fweares withall
To loofe his life, or fet his mother free.

   Lewis. *Arthur* away, 'tis time to looke about.

            B   *Elian.*

Elian. Why how now dame, what is your courage
coold?

Conſt. No *Elianor*, my courage gathers ſtrength,
And hopes to lead both *Iohn* and thee as ſlaues :
And in that hope, I hale thee to the field.   [*Exeunt.*

Excurſions. Elianor *is reſcued by* Iohn, *and* Arthur *is
taken Priſoner.* Exeunt. *Sound Victory.*

Enter Iohn, Elianor, *and* Arthur *priſoner*, Philip *the*
Baſtard, Pembroke, Saliſbury, *and* Hubert de Burgh.

K. Iohn. Thus right triumphs, and *Iohn* triumphs in
right :
Arthur thou ſeeſt, *Fraunce* cannot bolſter thee :
Thy mothers pride hath brought thee to this fall.
But if at laſt nephew thou yeelde thy ſelfe
Into the gardance of thine vncle *Iohn*,
Thou ſhalt be vſed as becomes a Prince.

Arth. Vncle, my grandame taught her nephew this,
To beare captiuitie with patience.
Might hath preuaild, not right, for I am King
Of *England*, though thou weare the Diademe.

2. Elian. Sonne *Iohn*, ſoone ſhall we teach him to
forget
Theſe prowd preſumptions, and to know himſelfe.

K. Iohn. Mother, he neuer will forget his claime,
I would he liude not to remember it.
But leauing this, we will to *England* now,
And take ſome order with our Popelings there,
That ſwell with pride and fat of lay mens lands.
Philip, I make thee chiefe in this affaire,

Ranſacke

Ranfacke the Abbeis, Cloyfters, Priories,
Conuert their coine unto my fouldiers vfe:
And whatfoere he be within my land,
That goes to *Rome* for iuftice and for law,
While he may haue his right within the realme,
Let him be iudgde a traitor to the ftate,
And fuffer as an enemy to *England*.
Mother, we leaue you here beyond the feas,
As Regent of our prouinces in *Fraunce*,
While we to *England* take a fpeedy courfe,
And thanke our God that gaue vs victorie.
Hubert de Burgh take *Arthur* here to thee,
Be he thy prifoner: *Hubert* keep him fafe,
For on his life doth hang thy Soueraignes Crowne,
But in his death confifts thy Soueraignes bliffe:
Then *Hubert*, as thou fhortly hearft from me,
So vfe the prifoner I haue giuen in charge.

  Hub. Frolicke yong prince, thogh I your keeper be,
Yet fhall your keeper liue at your command.

  Arth. As pleafe my God, fo fhall become of me.

  Q. Elian. My fonne, to *England*, I will fee thee fhipt,
And pray to God to fend thee fafe afhore.

  Phil. Now warres are done, I long to be at home,
To diue into the monks and abbots bagges,
To make fome fport among the fmooth fkind nunnes,
And keep fome reuel with the fanzen friers.

  K. Iohn. To *England* Lords, each looke vnto your
    charge,
And arm your felues againft the Roman pride. [*Exeunt.*

E 2   *Enter*

Enter the King of Fraunce, Lewis *his sonne,* Cardinall
Pandolph *Legate, and* Conſtance.

K. Phil. What, euery man attacht with this miſhap?
Why frowne you ſo, why droop ye Lords of *Fraunce?*
Me thinkes it differs from a warre like minde,
To lowre it for a checke or two of chaunce.
Had *Limoges* eſcapt the baſtards ſpight,
A little ſorrow might haue ſerude our loſſe.
Braue *Auſtria,* heauen ioyes to haue thee there.
    Pand. His ſoule is ſafe and free from purgatorie,
Our holy father hath diſpenſt his ſinnes,
The bleſſed ſaints haue heard our oriſons,
And all are mediators for his ſoule,
And in the right of theſe moſt holy warres,
His holineſſe free pardon doth pronounce
To all that follow you gainſt *Engliſh* heretikes,
Who ſtand accurſed in our mother church.

Enter Conſtance *alone.*

    K. Phil. To aggrauate the meaſure of our greefe,
All male-content comes *Conſtance* for her ſonne.
Be breefe good Madam, for your face imports
A tragicke tale behind thats yet vntold.
Her paſſions ſtop the organ of her voyce,
Deep ſorrow throbbeth miſ-befäln euents,
Out with it Ladie, that our act may end
A full cataſtrophe of ſad laments.
    Conſt. My tougue is tun'd to ſtorie forth miſhap:
When did I breathe to tell a pleaſing tale?

                                                    Muſt

Muſt *Conſtance* ſpeake ? let teares preuent her talke :
Muſt I diſcourſe ? let *Dido* ſigh and ſay,
She weepes again to heare the wracke of *Troy* :
Two words will ſerue, and then my tale is done :
Elianors proud brat hath rob'd me of my ſonne.

Lewis. Haue patience Madame, this is chance of warre :
He may be ranſom'd, we reuenge his wrong.

Conſt. Be it ne'er ſo ſoon, I ſhall not liue ſo long.

K. Phil. Deſpaire not yet, come *Conſtance* go with me :
Theſe clouds will fleet, the day will cleare againe. [*Exeunt*

Pand. Now *Lewis*, thy fortune buds with happy ſpring,
Our holy Fathers prayers effecteth this.
Arthur is ſafe, let *Iohn* alone with him,
Thy title next is fairſt to *Englands* crowne :
Now ſtirre thy father to begin with *Iohn*,
The Pope ſays I, and ſo is *Albion* thine.

Lewis. Thanks my Lord Legate for your good conceit :
Tis beſt we follow now the game is faire,
My father wants to worke him your good words.

Pand. A few will ſerue to forward him in this,
Thoſe ſhall not want : but let's about it then. [*Exeunt*

Enter Philip *leading a Friar, charging him to ſhew where the Abbots gold lay.*

Phil. Come on you fat Franciſcan, dallie no longer,
but ſhew me where the Abbots treaſure lies, or die.

Friar. *Bencaicamus Domini*, was euer ſuch an iniurie?
Sweet S. *Witbold* of thy lenitie, defend vs from extremitie,
And heare us for S. Charitie, oppreſſed with auſteritie.
In nomine Domini, make I my homily,
Gentle gentilitie grieue not the Cleargie.

E 3   *Phil.*

Phil. Gray-gown'd good face, coniure ye,
  Nere truft me for a groat,
If this waft girdle hang thee not
  That girdeth in thy coat.
Now bald and barefoot *Bungie* birds,
  When vp the gallowes climing,
Say *Philip* he had words enough,
  To put you downe with riming.
Fr. O pardon, O *parce*,
S. *Francis* for mercie,
Shall fhield thee from night-fpels,
And dreaming of diuels,
If thou wilt forgiue me,
And neuer more grieue me,
With fasting and praying,
And *Haile Marie* faying,
From black purgatorio,
A penance right forye:
Friar *Thomas* will warm you
It fhall neuer harm you.
Phil. Come leaue off your rabble,
  Sirs, hang up this lozell.
2d *Fr.* For charitie I beg his life,
  Saint *Francis* chiefeft friar,
The beft in all our Couent fir,
  To keep a vintners fire.
O ftrangle not the good old man,
  My hofteffe oldeft gueft,
And I will bring you by and by
  Vnto the Priors cheft.

                                    PHI.

Phil. I, faiſt thou ſo, and if thou wilt the Friar is at
liberty, if not, as I am honeſt man, I hang you both for
company.

 Fr. Come hither, this is the cheſt,
  Thogh ſimple to behold,
 That wanteth not a thouſand pound
  In ſiluer and in gold.
 My ſelf wil warrant ſul ſo much,
  I know the Abbots ſtore,
 Ile pawn my life there is no leſs,
  To haue what ere is more.
 Phil. I take thy word, the ouerplus
  Vnto thy ſhare ſhall come,
 But if there want of full ſo much,
  Thy necke ſhall pay the ſumme.
Breake vp the coffer, Friar.

 Fr. Oh I am undone, fair *Alice* the Nunne
Hath took up her reſt in the Abbots cheſt,
Sancte Benedicite, pardon my ſimplicitie.
Fie *Alice,* confeſſion will not ſalue this tranſgreſſion

 Phil. What haue we here, a holy Nunne?
  So keep me God in health.
 A ſmooth facde Nunn (for aught I know)
  Is all the Abbots wealth.
 Is this the Nunries chaſtitie?
  Beſhrew me but I thinke
 They go as oft to venery
  As niggards to their drinke.
 Why paltry Friar and Pandar too,
  Ye ſhameleſſe ſhauen crowne,
 Is this the cheſt that held a hoord,
  At leaſt a thouſand pound?

          And

And is the hoord a holy whore?
  Well, be the hangman nimble,
He'l take the pain to pay you home,
  And teach you to diffemble.
Nunne, O fpare the Friar *Anthony,*
  A better neuer was.
To fing a dirige folemnely,
  Or read a morning maffe.
If money be the meanes of this,
  I know an ancient Nunne,
That hath a hoord thefe feuen yeeres,
  Did neuer fee the funne;
And that is yours, and what is ours,
  So fauour now be fhowne,
You fhall commaund as commonly,
  As if it were your owne.
Fr. Your honour excepted.
Nunne. I *Thomas,* I meane fo.
Phil. From all faue from Friars.
Nunne. Good fir, doe not thinke fo.
Phil. I thinke and fee fo!
  Why how camft thou here?
Fr. To hide her from lay men.
Nunne. 'Tis true fir, for feare.
Phil. For fear of the laitie: a pitifull dred
When a Nunne flies for fuccour to a fat Friars bed.
But now for your ranfome my cloyfter-bred conney,
To the cheft that you fpeake of where lies fo much mony.
  Nunne. Faire fir, within this preffe, of plate and
    money is
The valew of a thoufand markes, and other thing by gis.
Let us alone, and take it all, tis yours fir, now you
    know it.
                                                    Phil.

Phil. Come on fir Friar, picke the locke, this geere
    doth cotton hanfome,
That couetoufneffe fo cunningly muft pay the lechers
    ranfome.
What is in the hoord?
  Fr. Friar *Laurence* my Lord, now holy water helpe vs,
Some witch or fome diuell is fent to delude us:
Haud credo Laurentius, that thou fhouldft be pend thus
In the preffe of a Nunne we are all vndone,
And brought to difcredence, if thou be Friar *Laurence.*
  Fr. Amor vincit omnia, fo *Cato* affirmeth,
And therefore a Friar whofe fancie foone burneth,
Becaufe he is mortall and made of mould,
He omits what he ought, and doth more than he fhquld.
  Phil. How goes this geere? the Friars cheft filld with
    a faufen Nunne.
The Nunne again locks Friar up
    To keep him from the funne.
Belike the preffe is Purgatorie,
    Or penance paffing grieuous:
The Friars cheft a hell for Nunnes!
    How do thefe dolts deceiue ys?
Is this the labour of their liues,
    To feede and liue at eafe?
To reuel fo lafciuioufly,
    As often as they pleafe.
Ile mend the fault, or fault my aime,
    If I do miffe amending,
Tis better burn the Cloyfters downe,
    Than leaue them for offending.
But holy you, to you I fpeake,
    To you religious diuell,

Is this the preſſe that holds the ſumme,
    To quit you for your euill?
Nunne. I crie *peccaui, parce me,*
    Good ſir I was beguil'd.
Fr. Abſolue ſir for charitie,
    Shee would be reconcil'd.
Phil. And ſo I ſhall, ſirs bind them faſt,
    This is their abſolution,
Goe hang them vp for hurting them,
    Haſte them to execution.
    Fr. Laurence. O *tempus edax rerum,*
Giue children bookes they teare them.
O *vanitas vanitatis,* in this waning *ætatis,*
At threeſcore welneere, to go to this geeſe,
To my conſcience a clog, to die like a dog.
Exaudi me Domine, ſuis me parce
Dabo pecuniam, ſi habeo veniam.
To goe and fetch it, I will diſpatch it,
A hundred pounds ſterling, for my liuesſparing.

    Enter Peter *a prophet, with people.*

Pet. Hoe, who is here? S. *Francis* be your ſpeed,
    Come in my flocke, and follow me,
Your fortunes I will reed,
    Come hither boy, go get thee home,
And clime not ouer hie,
For from aloft thy fortune ſtands,
    In hazard thou ſhalt die.
    Boy. God be with you *Peter,* I pray you come to our
houſe a Sunday.
                                              Pe.

Pet. My boy shew me thy hand, blesse thee my boy,
For in thy palme I see a many troubles are ybent to dwel,
But thou shalt scape them all and do full well.

Boy. I thank you *Peter*, there's a cheese for your labor:
my sister prays yee to come home, and tell her how many
husbands she shall haue, and shee'l giue you a rib of
bacon.

Pet. My master stays at the townes end for me, Ile
come to you all anone : I must dispatch some busines
with a Friar, and then Ile read your fortunes.

Phil. How now, a prophet! sir prophet whence are ye?

Pet. I am of the world and in the world, but liue not
as others, by the world: what I am I knbw, and what
thou.wilt be I know. If thou knoweft me now, be an-
swered: if not, enquire no more what I am.

Phil. Sir, I know you will be a dissembling knaue,
that deludes the people with blinde prophecies : you are
hee I look for, you shal away with me : bring away all
the table, and you Friar *Laurence*, remember your ran-
some a hundred pound, and a pardon for your selfe, and
the rest ; come on sir prophet, you shall with me to receiue a prophets rewarde.   [*Exeunt,*

Enter Hubert de Burgh *with three men.*

Hub. My masters, I haue shewed you what warrant
I haue for this attempt ; I perceiue by your heauy coun-
tenances, you had rather be otherwise imployed, and for
my owne part, I would the King had made choice of
some other executioner : only this is my comfort, that a
King commaunds, whose precepts neglected or omitted,
threatneth torture for the default. Therefore in briefe,
leaue

leaue me, and be ready to attend the aduenture: ftay
within that entry, and when you heare me crie, *God faue
the King*, iffue fodainely forth, lay hands on *Arthur*, fet
him in this chaire, wherein (once faft bound) leaue him
with me to finifh the reft.

Attendants. We goe, though loath.   [*Exeunt*
    Hub. My Lord, will it pleafe your honor to take the
benefit of the faire euening?

Enter Arthur *to* Hubert de Burgh.

    Arth. Gramercie *Hubert* for thy care of me,
In or to whom reftraint is newly knowne,
The ioy of walking is fmall benefit,
Yet will I take thy offer with fmall thanks,
I would not loofe the pleafure of the eie.
But tell me curteous Keeper if thou can,
How long the King will haue me tarrie heere.
    Hub. I know not Prince, but as I geffe, not long,
God fend you freedome, and *God faue the King*.

They iffue forth.

    Arth. Why how now firs, what may this outrage
        meane?
O helpe me *Hubert*, gentle keeper help,
God fend this fodaine mutinous approach
Tend not to reaue a wretched guiltles life.
    Hub. So firs, depart, and leaue the reft for me.
    Arth. Then *Arthur* yeeld, death frowneth in thy face,
What meaneth this? good *Hubert* pleade the cafe.
                                                Hub.

Hub. Patience yong Lord, and liften words of woe,
Harmefull and harſh, hells horror to be heard :
A diſmall tale fit for a furies tongue.
I fainte to tell, deepe ſorrow is the ſound.

Arth. What, muſt I die?

Hub. No newes of death, but tidings of more hate,
A wrathfull doome, and moſt unluckie fate :
Deaths diſh were daintie at ſo fell a feaſt,
Be deafe, hear not, its hell to tell the reſt.

Arth. Alas, thou wrongſt my youth with words of feare,
Tis hell, tis horror, not for one to heare:
What is it man if it muſt needes be done,
Act it, and end it, that the paine were gone.

Hub. I will not chaunt ſuch dolour with my tongue,
Yet muſt I act the outrage with my hand.
My heart, my head, and all my powers beſide,
To aide the office haue at once denide.
Peruſe this letter, lines of trebble woe,
Reade ore my charge, and pardon when you know.

> Hubert, *theſe are to commaund thee, as thou tendreſt our
> quiet in minde, and the eſtate of our perſon, that pre-
> ſently upon the receipt of our commaund, thou put out
> the eies of* Arthur Plantaginet.

Arth. Ah monſtrous damned man ! his very breath
infects the elements.
Contagious venome dwelleth in his heart,
Effecting meanes to poyſon all the world.
Vnreuerent may I be to blame the heauens
Of great iniuſtice, that the miſcreant
Liues to oppreſſe the innocents with wrong.
Ah *Hubert !* makes he thee his inſtrument,

F

To found the trump that caufeth hell triumph?
Heauen weepes, the faints do fhed celeftiall teares,
They feare thy fall, and cite thee with remorfe,
They knocke thy confcience, mouing pitie there,
Willing to fence thee from the rage of hell:
Hell *Hubert*, truft me all the plagues of hell
Hang on performance of this damned deede.
This feale, the warrant of the bodies bliffe,
Enfureth Satan chieftaine of thy foule:
Subfcribe not *Hubert*, giue not Gods part away.
I fpeake not only for eies priuilege,
The chief exterior that I would enioy:
But for thy perill, farre beyond my paine,
Thy fweet foules loffe, more than my eies vaine lacke:
A caufe internall, and eternall too.
Aduife thee *Hubert*, for the cafe is hard,
To loofe faluation for a Kings reward.
    Hub. My Lord, a fubiect dwelling in the land
Is tied to execute the Kings commaund.
        Arth. Yet God commaunds whofe power reacheth
            further,
That no commaund fhould ftand in force to murther.
    Hub. But that fame Effence hath ordaind a law,
A death for guilt, to keepe the world in awe.
    Arth. I pleade, not guilty, treafonleffe and free.
    Hub. But that appeale my Lord concernes not me.
    Arth. Why thou art he that maift omit the perill.
    Hub. I, if my foueraigne would omit his quarrell.
    Arth. His quarrell is vnhallowed falfe and wrong.
    Hub. Then be the blame to whom it doth belong.
    Arth. Why thats to thee if thou as they proceede,
Conclude their iudgment with fo vile a deede.

                                            Hub.

Hub. Why then no execution can be lawfull,
If Iudges doomes muſt be reputed doubtfull.

Arth. Yes where in form of law in place and time,
The offender is conuicted of the crime.

Hub. My Lord, my Lord, this long expoſtulation,
Heapes up more griefe, than promiſe of redreſſe ;
For this I know, and ſo reſolude I end,
That ſubiects liues on Kings commands depend.
I muſt not reaſon why he is your foe,
But do his charge ſince he commaunds it ſo.

Arth. Then do thy charge, and charged be thy ſoul,
With wrongfull perſecution done this day.
You rowling eyes, whoſe ſuperficies yet
I doe behold with eies that nature lent:
Send forth the terror of your Mouers frowne,
To wreake my wrong vpon the murtherers
That rob me of your faire reflecting view:
Let hell to them (as earth they wiſh to me)
Be darke and direfull guerdon for their guilt,
And let the blacke tormenters of deep *Tartary*
Vpbraide them with this damned enterpriſe,
Inflicting change of tortures on their ſoules.
Delay not *Hubert,* my oriſons are ended,
Begin I pray thee, reaue me of my ſight :
But to performe a tragedie indeede,
Conclude the period with a mortall ſtab.
Conſtance farewell, tormenter come away,
Make my diſpatch the Tyrants feaſting day.

Hub. I faint, I feare, my conſcience bids deſiſt :
Faint did I ſay ? feare was it that I named :
My King commaunds, that warrant ſets me free :
But God forbids, and he commaundeth Kings,

That

That great Commaunder countercheckes my charge,
He ſtayes my hand, he maketh ſoft my heart.
Goe curſed tooles, your office is exempt,
Cheere thee yong Lord, thou ſhalt not looſe an eie,
Thogh I ſhould purchaſe it with loſſe of life.
Ile to the King, and ſay his will is done
And of the langor tell him thou art dead,
Goe in with me, for *Hubert* was not borne
To blinde thoſe lampes that nature poliſht ſo.

   Arth. *Hubert*, if euer *Arthur* be in ſtate,
Looke for amends of this receiued gift,
I tooke my eieſight by thy curteſie,
Thou lentſt them me, I will not be ingrate,
But now procraſtination may offend
The iſſue that thy kindneſſe vndertakes:
Depart we *Hubert* to preuent the worſt.   [*Exeunt.*

    Enter King Iohn, Eſſex, Saliſbury, Pembroke.

   K. Iohn. Now warlike followers, reſteth ought vndone
That may impeach us of fond ouerſight?
The *French* haue felt the temper of our ſwords,
Cold terror keepes poſſeſſion in their ſoules,
Checking their ouerdaring arrogance
For buckling with ſo great an ouermatch:
The arch prowd titled Prieſt of *Italy*,
That calls himſelfe grand Vicar under God,
Is buſied now with trentall obſequies,
Maſſe and months mind, dirge and I know not what,
To eaſe their ſoules in painefull purgatorie,
That haue miſcarried in theſe bloody warres.
Heard you not Lords when firſt his holineſſe

                         Had

Had Tidings of our small account of him,
How with a taunt vaunting vpon his toes,
He vrgde a reason why the *English* Affe
Difdaind the bleffed ordinance of *Rome?*
The title (reuerently might I inferre):
Became the Kings that earft haue borne the load,
The flauifh weight of that controlling Prieft:
Who at his pleafure temperd them like waxe
To carrie armes on danger of his curfe,
Banding their foules with warrants of his hand.
I grieue to thinke how Kings in ages paft
(Simply deuoted to the See of *Rome*)
Haue run into a thoufand acts of fhame.
But now for confirmation of our ftate,
Sith we haue proond the more than needfull branch
That did oppreffe the true well-growing ftocke,
It refteth we throughout our territories.
Be reproclaimed and inuefted King.

   Pemb. My Liege, that were to bufie men with doubts,
Once were you crownd, proclaimd, and with applaufe
Your citie ftreets haue ecchoed to the eare,
God faue the King, God faue our foueraigne *Iohn.*
Pardon my feare, my cenfure doth inferre
Your highneffe not depofde from regall ftate,
Would breed a mutinie in peoples mindes,
What it fhould meane to haue you crownd againe.

   K. Iohn. *Pembroke,* performe what I haue bid thee do,
Thou knowft not what induceth me to this.
Effex goe in, and Lordings all be gone
About this tafke, I will be crownd anone.

Enter Philip *the Baſtard:*

Phil. What newes, how do the Abbots cheſts ?
Are Friars fatter than the Nunnes are faire ?
What cheere with Church-men ? had they gold or no ?
Tell me, how hath thy office tooke effect ?

  Phil. My Lord, I haue performd your Highnes charge :
The eaſe-bred Abbots, and the bare-foot Friars,
The Monks, the Priors, and holy cloyſtred Nunnes,
Are all in health, and were my Lord in wealth,
Till I had tithde and tolde their holy hoords.
I doubt not when your Highneſſe ſees my prize,
You may proportion all their former pride.

  K. Iohn. Why ſo, now ſorts it *Philip* as it ſhould :
This ſmall intruſion into Abbey trunkes,
Will make the Popelings excommunicate,
Curſe, ban, and breathe out damned oriſons,
As thicke as haile-ſtones fore the ſprings approach :
But yet as harmleſſe and without effect,
As is the eccho of a Cannons cracke
Diſchargde againſt the battlements of heauen.
But what news elſe befell there *Philip* ?

  Phil. Strange news my Lord: within your territories
Neere *Pomfret* is a prophet now ſprung up,
Whoſe diuination vollies wonders foorth :
To him the commons throng with countrey gifts,
He ſets a date unto the Beldames death,
Preſcribes how long the Virgins ſtate ſhall laſt,
Diſtinguiſheth the moouing of the heauens,
Giues limits vnto holy nuptiall rites,
Foretelleth famine, aboundeth plentie forth :

Of

Of fate, of fortune, life and death he chats,
With such assurance, scruples put apart,
As if he knew the certaine doomes of heauen,
Or kept a register of all the destinies.

    K. Iohn. Thou telst me maruels, would thou hadst
      brought the man,
We might haue questioned him of things to come.

    Phil. My Lord, I took a care of had-I-wist.
And brought the prophet with me to the court,
He staies my Lord but at the presence doore:
Pleaseth your Highnesse, I will call him in.

    K. Iohn. Nay stay awhile, wee'l haue him here anone.
A thing of weight is first to be perform'd.

Enter the nobles and crowne King Iohn, *and then cry,* God
saue the King.

    K. Iohn. Lordings and friends supporters of our state,
Admire not at this vnaccustomd course,
Nor in your thoughts blame not this deede of yours,
Once ere this time was I inuested King,
Your fealtie sworne as liegemen to our state:
Once since that time ambitious weedes haue sprung
To staine the beauty of our garden plot:
But heauens in our conduct rooting thence
The false intruders, breakers of worlds peace,
Haue to our ioy, made sun-shine chase the storme,
After the which, to trie your constancie,
That now I see is worthie of your names,
We crau'd once more your helpes for to inuest vs,
Into the right that envy thought to wracke.
Once was I not deposde, your former choice;
Now twice been crowned and applauded King?

                        Your

Your cheered action to install me so,
Infers assured witnesse of your loues,
And binds me ouer in a kingly care
To render loue with loue, rewards of worth
To ballance down requitall to the full.
But thankes the while, thankes Lordings to you all:
Aske me and vse me, trie me and finde me yours.

   Essex. A boone my Lord, at vantage of your words
We aske to guerdon all our loyalties.

   Pemb. We take the time your highnesa bids vs aske:
Pleafe it you grant, you make your promife good,
With lesser losse than one superfluous haire
That not remembred falleth from your head.

   K. Iohn. My word is past, receiue your boone my Lords,
What may it be? aske it, and it is yours.

   Essex. We craue my Lord, to pleafe the commons with
The libertie of Lady *Conftance* fonne:
Whofe durance darkeneth your Highneffe right,
As if you kept him prifoner, to the end
Your felfe were doubtfull of the thing you haue.
Difmiffe him thence, your Highneffe needs not feare,
Twice by confent you are proclaim'd our King.

   Pemb. This if you grant, were all vnto your good:
For fimple people mufe you keepe him clofe.

   K. Iohn. Your words haue fearcht the center of my
       thoughts,
Confirming warrant of your loyalties.
Difmiffe your counfell, fway my ftate,
Let *Iohn* doe nothing, but by your confents.
Why how now *Philip*, what extafie is this?
Why cafts thou up thy eyes to heauen fo?

                             Phil.

There the fiue Moones appeare.

Phil. See, fee, my Lord, ftrange apparitions,
Glancing mine eie to fee the diadem
Plac'd by the Bifhops on your Highneffe head,
From forth a gloomie cloud, which curtain-like
Difplaid itfelfe, I fuddainely efpied,
Fiue moones reflecting, as you fee them now :
Euen in the moment that the crowne was plac'd
Gan they appeare, holding the courfe you fee.

K. Iohn. What might portend thefe apparitions,
Vnvfual fignes, forerunners of euent,
Prefagers of ftrange terrors to the world ?
Beleeue me Lords, the obiect feares me much.
Philip thou toldft me of a Wizard but of late,
Fetch in the man to defcant of this fhow.

Pemb. The heauens frowne vpon the finfull earth,
When with prodigious vnaccuftom'd fignes
They fpot their fuperficies with fuch wonder.
Effex. Before the ruines of *Jerufalem,*
Such meteors were the Enfignes of his wrath,
That haft'ned to deftroy the faultfull towne.

Enter Philip *the Baftard with the Prophet.*

K. Iohn. Is this the man?
Phil. It is my Lord.
K. Iohn. Prophet of *Pomfret,* for fo I heare thou art,
That calculat'ft of many things to come :
Who by a power repleat with heauenly gift,
Canft blab the counfell of thy makers will,
If fame be true, or truth be wrong'd by thee,
                                        Decide

Decide in cyphering, what thefe fiue moones
Portend this clime, if they prefage at all.
Breath out thy gift, and if I liue to fee
Thy diuination take a true effect,
Ile honour thee aboue all earthly men.'

    Pet. The fkie wherein thefe moones haue refidence,
Prefenteth *Rome* the great *Metropolis,*
Where fits the Pope in all his holy pompe.
Foure of the moones prefent foure prouinces,
To wit, *Spaine, Denmarke, Germanie,* and *Fraunce,*
That beare the yoke of proud commanding *Rome,*
And ftand in feare to tempt the Prelates curfe.
The fmalleft moone that whirles about the reft,
Impatient of the place he holds with them,
Doth figure forth this ifland *Albion,*
Who gins to fcorne the fee and feat of *Rome,*
And feekes to fhunne the edicts of the Pope:
This fhowes the heauen, and this I do auerre
Is figured in the apparitions.

    K. Iohn. Why then it feemes the heauens fmile on vs,
Giuing applaufe for leauing of the Pope.
But for they chance in our Meridian,
Doe they effect no priuate growing ill
To be inflicted on vs in this clime?

    Pet. The moones effect no more than what I faid:
But on fome other knowledge that I haue
By my prefcience, ere Afcenfion day
Haue brought the funne vnto his ufuall height
Of Crowne, Eftate, and Royall dignity,
Thou fhalt be clean difpoyl'd and difpoffeft.

    K. Iohn. Falfe dreamer, perifh with thy witched newes
Villaine thou woundft me with thy fallacies:

                      If

If it be true, die for thy tidings price;
If falfe, for fearing me with vaine fuppofe :
Hence with the witch, hels damned fecretarie.
Lock him vp fure : for by my faith I fweare,
True or not true, the Wizard fhall not liue.
Before Afcenfion day——who fhould be caufe hereof?
Cut off the caufe, and then the effect will die.
Tut, tut, my mercie ferues to maime my felfe,
The roote doth liue, from whence thefe thornes fpring vp,
I and my promife paft for his deliu'rie :
Frowne friends, faile faith, the diuell goe withall,
The brat fhall die, that terrifies me thus.
Pembroke and *Effex*, I recall my graunt,
I will not buy your fauours with my feare :
Nay murmurs not, my will is lawe enough,
I loue you well, but if I lou'd you better,
I would not buy it with my difcontent.

Enter Hubert.

How now, what newes with thee ?
    Hub. According to your Highneffe ftrict commaund,
Young *Arthurs* eies are blinded and extinct.
    K. Iohn. Why fo, then he may feele the crown, but
        neuer fee it.
    Hub. Nor fee nor feele, for of the extreme paine,
Within one houre gaue he vp the ghoft.
    K. Iohn. What is he dead ?
    Hub. He is my Lord.
    K. Iohn. Then with him die my cares.
    Effex. Now ioy betide thy foule.
    Pemb. And heauens reuenge thy death.

                                                    Effex.

Effex. What haue you done my Lord? was euer heard
A deede of more inhumane confequence?
Your foes will curfe, your friends will crie reuenge.
Vnkindly rage, more rough than northern wind,
To clip the beautie of fo fweete a flower!
What hope in vs for mercie on a fault,
When kinfman dies without impeach of caufe,
As you haue done, fo come to cheere you with,
The gvilt fhall neuer be caft me in my teeth. *[Exeunt.*

K. Iobn. And are you gone? the diuell be your guide:
Proud rebels as ye are, to braue me fo:
Saucie, unciuill, checkers of my will.
Your tongues giue edge vnto the fatall knife,
That fhall haue paffage through your trayt'rous throats,
But hufh, breath not bugs words too foone abroad,
Left time preuent the iffue of thy reach.
Arthur is dead, I there the corzie growes:
But while he liu'd the danger was the more;
His death hath freed me from a thoufand feares,
But it hath purchas'd me ten times ten thoufand foes.
Why all is one, fuch lucke fhall haunt his game,
To whom the diuell owes an open fhame:
His life a foe that leueld at my crowne,
His death a frame to pull my building downe.
My thoughts harpt ftill on quiet by his end,
Who liuing aimed fhrewdly at my roome:
But to preuent that plea, twice was I crown'd,
Twice did my fubieds fweare me fealtie,
And in my confcience lou'd me as their liege,
In whofe defence they would haue pawn'd their liues.
But now they fhun me as a Serpents fting,
A tragyke tyrant, fterne and pitileffe,

And

And not a title followes after *Iohn*,
But butcher, blood-fucker, and murderer:
What planet gouern'd my natiuitie,
To bode me foueraigne types of high eftate,
So interlac'd with hellifh difcontent,
Wherein fell furie hath no intereft?
Curft be the crowne, chief author of my care,
Nay curft my will, that made the crowne my care:
Curft be my birth-day, curft ten times the wombe
That yeelded me aliue into the world.
Art thou the uillaine? Furies haunt thee ftill,
For killing him whom all the world laments.

    Hub. Why here's my Lord your highnes hand and feale,
Charging on liues regard to do the deed.

    K. Iohn. Ah dull conceipted peafant, knowft thou not
It was a damned execrable deed?
Shewft me a Seale? Oh villaine, both our foules
Haue folde their freedome to the thrall of hell,
Vnder the warrant of that curfed Seale.
Hence villaine, hang thy felfe, and fay in hell
That I am comming for a kingdome there.

    Hub. My Lord, attend the happy tale I tell,
For heauens health fend Sathan packing hence,
That inftigates your Highneffe to defpaire.
If *Arthurs* death be difmall to be heard,
Bandie the newes for rumors of untruth:
He liues my Lord, the fweeteft youth aliue,
In health, with eie fight, not a haire amiffe.
This heart tooke vigor from this forward hand,
Making it weake to execute your charge.

G

K. Iohn.

K. Iohn. What, liues he! then sweete hope come home
agen,
Chase hence despaire, the purueyor for hell.
Hye *Hubert,* tell these tidings to my Lords
That throb in passions for yong *Arthurs* death :
Hence *Hubert,* stay not till thou hast reueald
The wished news of *Arthurs* happy health.
I goe my selfe, the ioyfullst man aliue
To storie out this new supposed crime.   [*Exeunt.*

The End of the FIRST PART.

To the GENTLEMEN READERS.

T H E changelesse purpose of determinde Fate
    Giues period to our care, or hearts content;
When heauens fixt time for this or that hath end :
Nor can earths pomp or pollicie preuent
The doome ordained in their secret will.
    Gentles, we left King *Iohn* repleate with blisse
That *Arthur* liude, whom he supposed slaine ;
And *Hubert* posting to returne those Lords,
Who deem'd him dead, and parted discontent :
Arthur himselfe begins our latter Act,
Our Act of outrage, desprate furie, death ;
Wherein fond rashnesse murdreth first a Prince,
And Monkish falsenesse poysneth last a King.
First Scene shews *Arthurs* death in infancie,
And last concludes *Iohns* fatal tragedie.

The

The Second Part of

THE

Troublesome RAIGNE

OF

KING IOHN.

CONTAINING,

The Entrance of Lewis *the* French *Kings* ſonne : *with the Poyſoning of King* Iohn *by a Monke.*

Enter yong Arthur *on the walls.*

NOW help good hap to further mine entent,
  Croſſe not my youth with any more extremes :
  I venter life to gaine my libertie,
And if I die, worlds troubles haue an end.
Feare gins diſſwade the ſtrength of my reſolue,
My holde will faile, and then alas I fall,
And if I fall, no queſtion death is next :
Better deſiſt, and liue in priſon ſtill.
Priſon ſaid I ? nay, rather death than ſo :
Comfort and courage come againe to me,
Ile venter ſure : tis but a leape for life.

He leapes, and brufing his bones, after he was from his
traunce, fpeakes thus ;

Hoe, who is nigh ? fome bodie take me vp.
Where is my mother ? let me fpeake with her.
Who hurts me thus ? fpeake hoe, where are you gone ?
Ay me poore *Arthur*, I am heere alone.
Why calld I mother, how did I forget ?
My fall, my fall, hath killd my mothers fonne.
How will fhe weepe at tidings of my death ?
My death indeed, O God, my bones are burft.
Sweete *Iefu* faue my foule, forgiue my rafh attempt,
Comfort my mother, fhield her from defpaire,
When fhe fhall heare my tragycke ouerthrowe.
My heart controuls the office of my tongue,
My vital powers forfake my brufed trunke,
I die, I die, heauen take my fleeting foule,
And lady mother all good hap to thee.   *{He dies.*

Enter Pembroke, Saliſbury, and Effex.

Effex. My Lords of *Pembroke* and of *Saliſbury*,
We muft be careful in our policie,
To Vndermine the keepers of this place,
Elfe fhall we neuer find the Princes graue.

Pemb. My Lord of *Effex*, take no care for that,
I warrant you it was not clofely done.
But who is this ? lo Lords the withered flowre,
Who in his life fhin'd like the Mornings blufh,
Caft out a doore, deni'd his buriall right,
A prey for birds and beafts to gorge vpon.

Saliſb. O ruthfull fpectacle ! O damned deed !
My finews fhake, my very heart doth bleed.

                                        Effex.

Essex. Leaue childish teares braue Lords of *England*,
If water-floods could fetch his life againe,
My eies should conduit forth a sea of teares.
If sobs would helpe, or sorows serue the turne,
My heart should volley out deepe piercing plaints.
But bootlefs were't to breath as many sighes
As might ecclipfe the brighteft Sommers sunne,
Here refts the helpe, a seruice to his ghoft.
Let not the tyrant causer of this dole,
Liue to triumph in ruthfull maffacres,
Giue hand and heart, and *Englishmen* to armes,
Tis Gods decree to wreake us of these harmes,
 Pemb. The beft aduice: but who comes pofting here?

Enter Hubert.

Right noble Lords, I fpeake vnto you all,
The King entreats your fooneft fpeed
To vifit him, who on your prefent want,
Did ban and curfe his birth, himfelfe and me,
For executing of his ftrict commaund.
I faw his paffion, and at fitteft time,
Affur'd him of his coufins being fafe,
Whom pity would not let me doe to death:
He craues your company my Lords in hafte,
To whom I will conduct young *Arthur* ftraight,
Who is in health under my cuftody.
 Essex. In health bafe villaine, were't not I leaue the crime
To Gods reuenge, to whom reuenge belongs,
Here should'ft thou perish on my rapier's point.
Call'ft thou this health? fuch health betide thy friends,

And

And all that are of thy condition.

Hub. My Lords, but heare me fpeake, and kil me then,
If here I left not this yong Prince aliue,
Maugre the haftie Edict of the King,
Who gaue me charge to put out both his eyes,
That God that gaue me liuing to this houre,
Thunder reuenge vpon me in this place:
And as I tendred him with earneft loue,
So God loue me, and then I fhall be well.

Salifb. Hence traytor hence, thy counfel is herein.
                                                    [*Exit Hub.*

Some in this place appointed by the King,
Haue thrown him from his lodging here aboue,
And fure the murther hath bin newly done,
For yet the body is not fully cold.

Effex. How fay you Lords, fhall we with fpeed difpatch
Vnder our hands a packet into *Fraunce,*
To bid the Dolphin enter with his force,
To claime the kingdom for his proper right,
His title maketh lawful ftrength thereto.
Befides the Pope, on peril of his curfe,
Hath bard us of obedience vnto *Iohn,*
This hateful murder, *Lewis* his true defcent,
The holy charge that we receiu'd from *Rome,*
Are weightie reafons, if you like my read,
To make us all perfeuer in this deed.

Pemb. My Lord of *Effex,* well haue you admis'd,
I will accord to further you in this.

Salifb. And *Salifbury* will not gainefay the fame:
But aid that courfe as farre forth as he can.

Effex. Then each of vs fend ftraight to his allies,

                                                    To

To win them to this famous enterprise :
And let us all yclad in Palmers weed,
The tenth of April at S. Edmunds Bury
Meet to conferre, and on the altar there
Swear secrecie and aide to this aduise.
Mean while, let vs conuey this body hence,
And giue him buriall, as befits his state,
Keeping his monthes mind, and his obsequies,
With solemne intercession for his soule.
How say you Lordings, are you all agreed?

   Pemb. The tenth of April at S. *Edmunds Burie*,
God letting not, I will not faile the time.

    Essex. Then let vs all conuey the body hence. [*Exeunt.*

Enter K. Iohn, *with two or three, and* Peter *the Prophet.*

   K. Iohn. Disturbed thoughts, foredoomers of mine ill
Distracted passions, signes of growing harmes,
Strange prophecies of imminent mishaps,
Counfound my wits, and dull my senses so,
That euery obiect these mine eies behold,
Seeme instruments to bring me to my end.
Ascension day is come, Iohn feare not then
The prodigies this pratling Prophet threats.
Tis come indeed : ah were it fully past,
Then were I carelesse of a thousand feares.
The diall tells me it is twelue at noone.
Were twelue at midnight past, then might I vaunt,
False seers prophecies of no import.
Could I as well with this right hand of mine
Remoue the Sunne from our Meridian,
Vnto the moonested circle of th' antipodes,

                  A3

As turn this fteele from twelue to twelue agen,
Then *Iohn,* the date of fatall prophecies,
Should with the Prophets life together end.
But *multa cadunt inter calicem fupremaque labra.*
Peter, vnfay thy foolifh doting dreame,
And by the crowne of *England* here I fweare,
To make thee great, and greateft of thy kin.

  Pet. King *Iohn,* although the time I haue prefcrib'd
Be but twelue hours remaining yet behind,
Yet do I know by infpiration,
Ere that fixt time be fully come about,
King *Iohn* fhall not be King as heretofore.

  K. Iohn. Vaine buzzard, what mifchance can chance
      fo foone,
To fet a King befide his regall feat?
My heart is good, my body paffing ftrong,
My land in peace, my enemies fubdu'd,
Onely my barons ftorme at *Arthurs* death:
But *Arthur* liues, I there the challenge growes,
Were he difpatch'd vnto his longeft home,
Then were the King fecure of thoufand foes.
Hubert, what newes with thee, where are my Lords?

  Hub. Hard newes my Lord, *Arthur* the lovely Prince,
Seeking to efcape ouer the caftle walles,
Fell headlong downe, and in the curfed fall.
He brake his bones, and there before the gate
Your barons found him dead, and breathleffe quite.

  K. Iohn. Is *Arthur* dead? then *Hubert* without more
      words hang the Prophet.
Away with *Peter,* villain out of my fight,
I am deafe, be gone, let him not fpeake a word.

                          Now

Now *Iohn* thy feares are vanisht into smoake,
Arthur is dead, thou guiltlesse of his death.
Sweet youth, but that I striued for a crowne,
I could haue well affoarded to thine age,
Long life and happinesse to thy content.

Enter Philip *the Baſtard.*

K. Iohn. *Philip* what news with thee ?
Phil. The news I heard was *Peters* prayers,
Who wisht like fortnne to befall vs all :
And with that werd, the rope his lateſt friend,
Kept him from falling headlong to the ground.
  K. Iohn. There let him hang, and be the rauens food,
While *Iohn* triumphs in ſpite of prophecies.
But whats the tidings from the Popelings now ?
What ſay the monks and priefts to our proceedings ?
Or where's the Barons that ſo sddainely
Did leaue the King upon a falſe ſurmiſt ?
  Phil. The Prelates ſteam and thirſt for ſharp reuenge :
But pleaſe your Maieſtie, were that the worſt,
It little skild : a greater danger growes,
Which muſt be weeded out by careful ſpeed,
Or all is loft, for all is leueld at.
  K. Iohn. More frights and feares ! what ere thy
      tidings be,
I am prepar'd : then *Philip,* quickly ſay,
Meane they to murder, or impriſon me ?
To giue my Crowne away to *Raine* or *Fraunce* ?
Or will they each of them become a King ?
Worſe than I think it is, it cannot be.
  Phil. Not worſe my Lord, but euery whit as bad.
                                        The

The nobles haue elected *Lewis* King,
In right of Lady *Blanch,* your neece, his wife :
His landing is expected euery houre,
The Nobles, Commons, Clergie, all Estates,
Incited, chiefly by the Cardinall,
Pandulph, that lies here Legate for the Pope,
Thinke long to see their new elected King.
And for undoubted proofe, see here my Liege,
Letters to me from your Nobilitie,
To be a partie in this action :
Who vnder shew of fained holinesse,
Appoint their meeting at S. *Edmunds Burie,*
There to consult, conspire, and conclude
The ouerthrow and downefall of your State.

    K. Iohn. Why so it must be : one houre of content,
Match'd with a month of passionate effects.
Why shines the Sunne to fauour this consort ?
Why do the winds not breake their brazen gates,
And scatter all these periur'd complices,
With all their counsels, and their damned drifts ?
But see the welkin rolleth gently on,
There's not a lowring cloud to frowne on them ;
The heauen, the earth, the sunne, the moone and all,
Conspire with those confederates my decay.
Then hell for me, if any power be there,
Forsake that place, and guide me step by step,
To poyson, strangle, murder in their steps
These traytors : oh that name is too good for them,
And death is easie : is there nothing worse,
T'o wreake me on this proud peace-breaking crew ?
What saist thou *Philip?* why assists thou not ?

                            Phil.

Phil. Thefe curfes (good my Lord) fit not the feafon :
Help muft defcend from heauen againft this treafon ?

K. Iohn. Nay thou wilt proue a traytor with the reft,
Goe get thee to them, fhame come to you all.

Phil. I would be loath to leaue your Highneffe thus,
Yet your commaund, and I, though grieu'd, will goe.

K. Iohn. Ah *Philip*, whither go'ft thou ? come againe.

Phil. My Lord, thefe motions are as paffions of a
mad man.

K. Iohn. A mad man *Philip*, I am mad indeed,
My heart is maz'd, my fences all foredone.
And *Iohn* of *England* now is quite vndone.
Was euer King as I oppreft with cares ?
Dame *Elianor* my noble mother Queene,
My only hope and comfort in diftreffe,
Is dead, and *England* excommunicate,
And I am interdicted by the Pope,
All Churches curft, their doores are fealed vp,
And for the pleafure of the Romifh Prieft,
The feruice of the Higheft is neglected,
The multitude (a beaft of many heads)
Doe wifh confufion to their foueraigne;
The nobles blinded with ambitions fumes,
Affemble powers to beat mine Empire downe :
And more than this, elect a forrein King.
O *England*, wert thou euer miferable,
King *Iohn* of *England* fees thee miferable :
Iohn, tis thy finnes that make it miferable,
Quicquid delirant Reges, plectuntur Achiui.
Philip, as thou haft euer lou'd thy King,
So fhow it now : poft to S. *Edmunds Burie*,

Diffemble

Diſſemble with the nobles, know their drifts,
Confound their diuelliſh plots, and damn'd deuiſes.
Though *Iohn* be faultie, yet let ſubiects beare,
He will amend, and right the peoples wrongs.
A mother, though ſhee were vnnaturall,
Is better than the kindeſt ſtep-dame is :
Let neuer *Engliſhman* truſt forreine rule.
Then *Philip* ſhew thy fealty to thy King,
And mongſt the Nobles plead thou for the King.

  Phil. I goe my Lord : ſee how he is diſtraught,
This is the curſed Prieſt of *Italy*
Hath heap'd theſe miſchiefs on this hapleſſe land.
Now *Philip*, hadſt thou *Tullies* eloquence,
Then might'ſt thou hope to plead with good ſucceſſe. [*Exit.*

  K. Iohn. And art thou gone ? ſucceſſe may follow thee :
Thus haſt thou ſhew'd thy kindneſſe to thy King.
Sirra, in haſte goe greet the Cardinall,
Pandulph I meane, the Legate from the Pope.
Say that the King deſires to ſpeake with him.
Now *Iohn* bethinke thee how thou maiſt reſolue :
And if thou wilt continue *Englands* King,
Then caſt about to keepe thy Diadem ;
For life and land, and all is leueld at.
The Pope of *Rome*, tis he that is the cauſe,
He curſeth thee, he ſets thy ſubiects free
From due obedience to their Soueraigne :
He animates the Nobles in their warres,
He giues away the Crowne to *Philips* ſonne,
And pardons all that ſeeke to murder thee :
And thus blind zeal is ſtill predominant.
Then *Iohn* there is no way to keepe thy crowne,
But finely to diſſemble with the Pope :

                                              That

That hand that gaue the wound muft giue the falue
To cure the hurt, elfe quite incurable.
Thy finnes are farre too great to be the man
T'abolifh Pope, and popery from thy Realme:
But in thy feate, if I may guefle at all,
A King fhall raigne that fhall fuppreffe them all.
Peace *Iohn*, here comes the Legate of the Pope,
Diffemble thou, and whatfoere thou fai'ft,
Yet with thy heart wifh their confufion.

Enter Pandulph.

Pand. Now *Iohn*, vnworthy man to breath on earth,
That do'ft oppugne againft thy mother Church:
Why am I fent for to thy curfed felf?

K. Iohn. Thou man of God, Vicegerent for the Pope,
The holy Vicar of S. *Peters* Church,
Vpon my knees, I pardon craue of thee,
And doe fubmit me to the fee of *Rome*,
And vow for penance of my high offence,
To take on me the holy crofs of Chrift,
And carry armes in holy Chriftian warres.

Pand. No *Iohn*, thy crowching and diffembling thus
Cannot deceiue the Legate of the Pope,
Say what thou wilt, I will not credite thee:
Thy Crowne and Kingdome both are tane away,
And thou art curft without redemption.

K. Iohn. Accurft indeed to kneele to fuch a drudge,
And get no help with thy fubmiffion!
Vnfheathe thy fword, and flay the mifprowd prieft
That thus triumphs ore thee a mightie King:
No *Iohn*, fubmit againe, diffemble yet,

H   For

For Priests and women must be flattered.   [*Aside.*
Yet holy Father thou thyselfe dost know,
No time too late for Sinners to repent,
Absolue me then, and *Iohn* doth sweare to do
The uttermost what euer thou demaundst.

   Pand. Iohn, now I see thy hearty penitence,
I rew and pity thy distrest estate,
One way is left to reconcile thy selfe,
And onely one, which I shall shew to thee.
Thou must surrender to the see of *Rome*
Thy Crowne and Diadem, then shall the Pope
Defend thee from th' inuasion of thy foes.
And where his Holinesse hath kindled *Fraunce,*
And set thy subiects hearts at warre with thee,
Then shall he curse thy foes, and beat them downe,
That seeke the discontentment of the King.

   K. Iohn. From bad to worse, or I must loose my realme,
Or giue my Crowne for penance vnto *Rome:*
A miserie more piercing than the darts
That breake from burning exhalations power.
What, shall I giue my Crowne with this right hand?
No: with this hand defend thy Crowne and thee.
What newes with thee?

Enter Meſſenger.

Pleaſe it your Maieſtie, there is deſcried on the coaſt of
Kent an hundred Sayle of Ships, which of all men is
thought to be the *French* fleet, vnder the conduct of
the *Dolphin*, ſo that it puts the countrey in a mu-
tiny, ſo they ſend to your Grace for ſuccour.

K. Iohn. How now, Lord Cardinal, what's your beſt
aduiſe ?

Theſe mutinies muſt be allaid in time,
By policy or headſtrong rage at leaſt.
O *Iohn*, theſe troubles tyre thy wearied ſoule,
And like to *Luna* in a ſad Eclipſe,
So are thy thoughts and paſſions for this newes.
Well may it be, when Kings are grieued ſo,
The vulgar ſort worke Princes ouerthrowe.

Pand. K. *Iohn*, for not effecting of thy plighted vow,
This ſtrange annoyance happens to thy Land:
But yet be reconcil'd vnto the Church,
And nothing ſhall be grieuous to thy ſtate.

K. Iohn. On *Pandulph*, be it as thou haſt decreed,
Iohn will not ſpurne againſt thy ſound aduiſe,
Come lets away, and with thy helpe I trow,
My Realme ſhall flouriſh, and my Crowne in peace.

Enter the Nobles, Pembroke, Eſſex, Cheſter, Bewchampe,
Clare, *with others.*

Pemb. Now ſweet S. *Edmund* holy Saint in heauen,
Whoſe Shrine is ſacred, high eſteem'd on earth,
Infuze a conſtant zeale in all our hearts,
To proſecute this act of mickle weight,
Lord *Bewchampe* ſay, what friends haue you procur'd.

Bewch.

Bewch. The Ld. *Fitzwater,* Ld. *Percie,* and Ld. *Rosse,*
Vow'd meeting here this day the leuenth houre.

Essex. Vnder the cloke of holy pilgrimage,
By that same houre on warrant of their faith,
Philip Plantagenet, a bird of swiftest wing,
Lord *Eustauce, Vescy,* Lord *Cressy,* and Lord *Mowbrey,*
Appointed meeting at S. *Edmunds* shrine.

Pemb. Vntill their presence, Ile conceale my tale,
Sweet complices in holy Christian acts,
That venture for the purchasse of renowne,
Thrice welcome to the league of high resolue,
That pawne their bodies for their soules regard.

Essex. Now wanteth but the rest to end this worke,
In Pilgrimes habite comes our holy troupe
A furlong hence, with swift vnwoonted pace,
May be they are the persons you expect.

Pemb. With swift vnwoonted gate, see what a thing is
    zeale,
That spurs them on with feruence to this shrine,
Now ioy come to them for their true intent:
And in good time, here come the war-men all,
That sweat in body by the minds disease:
Hap and hearts-ease braue Lordings be your lot.

Enter Philip *the Bastard,* &c.

Amen my Lords, the like betide your lucke,
And all that trauell in a Christian cause.

Essex. Cheerely repli'd braue branch of Kingly stocke,
A right *Plantagenet* should reason so.
But silence Lords, attend our commings cause:
The seruile yoke that pained vs with toyle,
On strong instinct hath fram'd this conuenticle,

To

To eafe our neckes of feruitudes contempt.
Should I not name the foeman of our reft,
Which of you all fo barren in conceipt,
As cannot leuell at the man I meane?
But left Enigmas fhadow fhining truth,
Plainely to paint, as truth requires no art,
Th'effect of this refort importeth this,
To root and clean extirpate tyrant *Iohn*,
Tyrant I fay, appealing to the man,
If any here, that loues him ; and I afke,
What kindfhip, lenitie, or Chriftian raigne,
Rules in the man to beare this foul impeach?
Firft I inferre the *Chefters* banifhment:
For reprehending him in moft vnchriftian crimes,
Was fpecial notice of a tyrants will.
But were this all, the diuell fhou'd be fau'd,
But this the leaft of many thoufand faults,
That circumftance with leifure might difplay.
Our priuate wrongs, no parcell of my tale
Which now in prefence, but for fome great caufe
Might wifh to him as to a mortall foe.
But fhall I clofe the period with an act
Abhorring in the eares of Chriftian men,
His coufins death, that fweete vnguiltie child,
Vntimely butcher'd by the tyrants meanes,
Here are my proofes, as cleere as grauel brooke,
And on the fame I further muft inferre,
That who vpholds a tyrant in his courfe,
Is culpable of all his damned guilt.
To fhew the which, is yet to be defcrib'd.
My Lord of *Pembroke*, fhew what is behinde,
Onely I fay, that were there nothing elfe.

To

To mooue vs, but the Popes most dreadfull curse,
Whereof we are assured, if we faile,
It were enough to instigate vs all,
With earnestnesse of spirit, to seeke a meane
To dispossesse *Iohn* of his regiment.

  Pemb. Well hath my Lord of *Essex* told his tale,
Which I auerre for most substantiall truth,
And more to make the matter to our minde,
I say that *Lewis* in challenge of his wife,
Hath title of an vncontrouled plea,
To all that longeth to our *English* crowne.
Short tale to make, the See Apostolike
Hath offered dispensation for the fault,
If any be, as trust me none I know,
By planting *Lewis* in the Vsurpers roome :
This is the cause of all our presence here,
That on the holy Altar we protest,
To aid the right of *Lewis* with goods and life,
Who on our knowledge is in armes for *England*:
What say you Lords?

  Salisb. As *Pembroke* faith, affirmeth *Salisbury* :
Faire *Lewis* of *Fraunce* that spoused Lady *Blanch*,
Hath title of an vncontrouled strength
To *England*, and what longeth to the crowne :
In right whereof, as we are true inform'd,
The Prince is marching hitherward in armes,
Our purpose, to conclude that with a word,
Is to inuest him as we may deuise,
King of our countrey, in the tyrants stead :
And so the warrant on the Altar sworne,
And so the intent for which we hither came.

  Phil. My Lord of *Salisbury*, I cannot couch

My

My speeches with the needful words of arte,
As doth beseeme in such a waightie worke,
But what my conscience and my duty will,
I purpose to impart,
For *Chesters* exile, blame his busie wit,
That medled where his dutie quite forbade :
For any priuate causes that you haue,
Me thinke they should not mount to such a height,
As to depose a King in their renenge.
For *Arthurs* death, K. *Iohn* was innocent,
He desperate was the deathsman to himselfe,
Which you, to make a colour to your crime,
Iniustly do impute it to his defalt,
But wher fel traitorisme hath residence,
There want no words to set despight on worke.
I say tis shame, and worthy all reproofe,
To wrest such petty wrongs in tearms of right,
Against a King annointed by the Lord.
Why *Salisbury*, admit the wrongs are true,
Yet subiects may not take in hand reuenge,
And rob the heauens of their proper power,
Where sitteth he to whom reuenge belongs.
And doth a pope, a priest, a man of pride,
Giue charters for the liues of lawfull Kings?
What can he blesse, or who regards his curse,
But such as giue to man, and take from God?
I speake it in the sight of God aboue,
There's not a man that dies in your beleefe,
But sells his soule perpetually to paine.
Aid *Lewis*, leaue God, kill *Iohn*, please hell,
Make hauocke of the welfare of your soules,
For here I leaue you in the sight of heauen,

A troope

A troope of traytors, food for hellish fiends :
If you defist, then follow me as friends,
If not, then do your worst, as hatefull traytors.
For *Lewis* his right, alasse tis too too lame,
A senslesse claime, if truth be titles friend,
In briefe, if this be cause of our resort,
Our pilgrimage is to the diuels shrine.
I came not Lords to troupe as traytors doe,
Nor will I counsell in so bad a cause :
Please you returne, we go againe as friends,
If not, I to my King, and you where traytors please. [*Exit.*

    Percie. A hot yong man, and so my Lords proceed,
I let him goe, and better lost than found.

    Pemb. What say you Lords, will all the rest proceed,
Will you all with me sweare vpon the Altar,
That you will to the death, be aid to *Lewis*, and enemy
       to *Iohn ?*
Euery man lay his hand by mine, in witnes of his harts
      accord.
Well then, euery man to armes to meet the King,
Who is already before *London.*

             Enter Messenger.

    Pemb. What newes Herauld ?
    The right Christian Prince my master, *Lewis* of
Fraunce, is at hand, comming to visit your Honours,
directed hither by the right honourable *Richard* Earle of
Bigot, to conferre with your honours.
    Pemb. How neere is his Highnesse ?
    Mess. Ready to enter your presence.

                             Enter

Enter Lewis, *Earle* Bigot, *with his troupe.*

Lewis. Faire Lords of *England*, *Lewis* salutes you all
As friends, and firm wel-willers of his weale,
At whose requeſt, from plentie flowing *Fraunce*,
Croſſing the Ocean with a ſoutherne gale,
He is in perſon come at your commaunds,
To vndertake and gratifie withall,
The fulneſſe of your fauours profferd him.
But worlds braue men, omitting promiſes,
Till time be miniſter of more amends,
I muſt acquaint you with our fortunes courſe.
The heauens dewing fauours on my head,
Haue in their conduct ſafe with victory,
Brought me along your well mannred bounds,
With ſmall repulſe, and little croſs of chance,
Your citie *Rochester*, with great applauſe,
By ſome diuine inſtinct laid armes aſide :
And from the hollow holes of *Thameſis*,
Eccho apace repli'd, *Viue le Roy.*
From thence, along the wanton rowling glade
To *Troynouant*, your faire *Metropolis*,
With lucke came *Lewix*, to ſhew his troupes of *Fraunce*,
Wauing our Enſignes with the dallying winds,
The fearfull obiect of fell frowning warre :
Where after ſome aſſault, and ſmall defence,
Heauens may I ſay, and not my warlike troupe,
Temperd their hearts to take a friendly foe
Within the compaſſe of their high built wals,
Giuing me title, as it ſeemd they wiſh.
Thus fortune (Lords) acts to your forwardneſſe,

Meanes

Meanes of content, in lieu of former griefe:
And may I liue but to requite you all,
Worlds wifh were mine, in dying noted yours.

   Salifb. Welcom the balme that clofeth vp our wounds,
The foueraigne medcine for our quicke recure,
The anchor of our hope, the onely prop,
Whereon depends our liues, our lands, our weale,
Without the which, as fheepe without their heird,
(Except a fhepheard winking at the wolfe)
We ftray, we pine, we run to thoufand harmes.
No maruell then, though with vnwonted ioy,
We welcome him that beateth woes away.

   Lewis. Thanks to you all of this religious league,
A holy knot of Catholike confent.
I cannot name you Lordings, man by man,
But like a ftranger vnacquainted yet,
In generall I promife faithfull loue:
Lord *Bigot* brought me to S. *Edmunds* fhrine,
Giuing me warrant of a Chriftian oath,
That this affembly came deuoted here,
To fweare according as your packets fhow'd,
Homage and loyall feruice to our felfe,
I need not doubt the furetie of your wils,
Since well I know, for many of your fakes,
The townes haue yeelded on their own accords:
Yet for a fafhion, not for mifbeleefe,
My eyes muft witneffe, and thefe eares muft heare
Your oath vpon the holy Altar fworne,
And after march, to end our commings caufe.

   Salifb. That we intend no other than good truth,
All that are prefent of this holy league,
For confirmation of our better truft,

                          In

In prefence of his Highneffe, fweare with me,
The fequel that my felfe fhall vtter here.

    I *Thomas Plantagenet*, Earle of *Salifbury*, fweare upon
the Altar, and by the holy army of Saints, homage and
allegeance to the right Chriftian Prince *Lewis* of *Fraunce*,
as true and rightfull King to *England*, *Cornewall* and
Wales, and to their territories: in the defence whereof
I vpon the holy Altar fweare all forwardneffe. *All the
Englifh Lords fweare.*

    Lords. As the noble Earle hath fworne, fo fweare we all.

    Lewis. I reft affured on your holy oath,
And on this Altar in like fort I fweare
Loue to you all, and princely recompence
To guerdon your good wils vnto the full.
And fince I am at this religious fhrine,
My good wel-willers giue vs leaue awhile,
To vfe fome orizons ourfelues apart,
To all the holy company of heauen,
That they will fmile vpon our purpofes,
And bring them to a fortunate euent.

    Salifb. We leaue your Highneffe to your good intent.

        Exeunt Lords of England.

    Lewis. Now vifcount *Meloun*, what remains behind?
Truft me thefe traytors to their Soueraigne State,
Are not to be beleeu'd in any fort.

    Meloun. Indeed my Lord, they that infringe their oaths,
And play the Rebels gainft their natiue King,
Will for as little caufe reuolt from you,
If euer opportunitie incite them fo:

                          For

For once forſworne, and neuer after found,
. There's no affiance after periury.

    Lewis. Wel, *Meloun*, wel, let's ſmooth with them awhile,
Vntil we haue as much as they can doe:
And when their vertue is exhaled drie,
Ile hang them for the guerdon of their helpe:
Meane while wee'l uſe them as a pretious poyſon,
To vndertake the iſſue of our hope.

    Fr. Lord. Tis policy (my Lord) to bait our hookes
With merry ſmiles, and promiſe of much weight:
But when your Highneſſe needeth them no more;
Tis good make ſure worke with them, leſt indeede
They prooue to you as to their naturall King.

    Meloun. Truſt mee my Lord, right well haue you aduiſed:
Venome for vſe, but neuer for a ſport
Is to be dallied with, leſt it infect.
Were you inſtalld, as ſoon I hope you ſhall :
Be free from traitors, and diſpatch them all.

    Lewis. That ſo I meane, I ſweare before you all
On this ſame Altar, and by heauens power,
There's not an *Engliſh* traitor of them all,
Iohn once diſpatcht, and I faire *Englands* King,
Shall on his ſhoulders beare his head one day,
But I will crop it for their guilts deſert :
Nor ſhall their heires inioy their Seigniories,
But periſh by their parents ſoule amiſſe.
This haue I ſworne, and this will I performe,
If ere I come unto the height I hope.
Lay downe your hands, and ſweare the ſame with me.

      The French Lords ſweare.

. . . Why ſo, now call them in, and ſpeake them faire,
  A ſmile of *Fraunce* will feede an *Engliſh* foole.

                        Beare

Beare them in hand as friends, for fo they be:
But in the heart like traytors as they are,

Enter the Englifh *Lords.*

Now famous followers, chiefetaines of the world,
Haue we follicited with hearty prayer
The heauen in fauour of our high attempt.
Leaue we this place, and march we with our power
To rowfe the tyrant from his chiefeft hold:
And when our labours haue a profprous end,
Each man fhall reape the fruit of his defert.
And fo refolu'd, braue followers let vs hence.   [*Exeunt.*

Enter King Iohn, Philip *the Baftard,* Pandulph, *and a many Priefts with them.*

Pand. Thus *Iohn,* thou art abfolu'd from all thy finnes,
And freed by order from our Fathers curfe.
Receiue thy Crowne againe, with this prouifo,
That thou remain true liegeman to the Pope,
And carry armes in right of holy *Rome.*
   K. Iohn. I holde the fame as tenant to the Pope,
And thanke your Holineffe for your kindneffe fhewne.
   Phil. A proper ieft, when Kings muft ftoop to Friars,
Need hath no law, when Friars muft be Kings.

Enter a Meffenger.

   Meff. Pleafe it your Maieftie, the Prince of *Fraunce,*
With all the Nobles of your Graces land
Are marching hitherward in good aray.
Where ere they fet their foot, all places yeeld :
                    I   Thy

Thy land is theirs, and not a foot holds out,
But *Douer* Castle, which is hard besieg'd.

' *Pand.* Feare not King *Iohn*, thy kingdome is the Popes,
And they shall know his Holinesse hath power,
To beate them soone from whence he hath to doe.

Drums and Trumpets. Enter Lewis, Meloun, Salisbury,
Essex, Pembroke, *and all the Nobles from* Fraunce *and*
England.

Lewis. Pandulph, as gaue his Holinesse in charge,
So hath the Delphin mustred vp his troupes,
And wonne the greatest part of all this land.
But ill becomes your Grace Lord Cardinall,
Thus to conuerse with *Iohn* that is accurst.

Pand. Lewis of *Fraunce,* victorious Conqueror,
Whose sword hath made this Iland quake for feare;
Thy forwardnesse to fight for holy *Rome,*
Shall be remunerated to the full:
But know my Lord, King *Iohn* is now absolu'd,
The Pope is pleasde, the land is blest agen,
And thou hast brought each thing to good effect.
It resteth then that thou withdraw thy powers,
And quietly return to *Fraunce* againe:
For all is done the Pope would wish thee doe.

Lewis. But all's not done that *Lewis* came to doe.
Why *Pandulph,* hath King *Philip* sent his sonne
And beene at such excessiue charge in warres,
To be dismist with words? King *Iohn* shall know,
England is mine, and he vsurps my right.

Pand. Lewis, I charge thee and thy complices
Vpon the paine of *Pandulphs* holy curse,

That

That thou withdraw thy powers to *Fraunce* againe,
And yeelde vp *London* and the neighbour townes
That thou haſt tane in *England* by the ſword.

   Meloun. Lord Cardinall, by *Lewis* princely leaue,
It can be nought but vſurpation
In thee, the Pope, and all the Church of *Rome*,
Thus to inſult on Kings of *Chriſtendome*,
Now with a word to make them carrie armes,
Then with a word to make them leaue their armes.
This muſt not be: Prince *Lewis* keepe thine owne,
Let Pope and Popelings curſe their bellies full.

   Phil. My Lord of *Meloun*, what title had the Prince
To *England* and the Crowne of *Albion*,
But ſuch a title as the Pope confirm'd:
The Prelate now lets fall his fained claime:
Lewis is but the agent for the Pope,
Then muſt the *Dolphin* ceaſe, ſith he hath ceaſt :
But ceaſe or no, it greatly matters not,
If you my Lords and Barons of the Land
Will leaue the *French*, and cleaue vnto our King,
For ſhame yee Peeres of *England* ſuffer not
Your ſelues, your honours, and your land to fall :
But with reſolued thoughts beate backe the *French*,
And free the Land from yoke of ſeruitude.

   Saliſb. *Philip*, not ſo, Lord *Lewis* is our King,
And we will follow him vnto the death.

   Pand. Then in the name of *Innocent* the Pope,
I curſe the Prince and all that take his part,
And excommunicate the rebell Peeres
As traitors to the King, and to the Pope.

   Lewis. Pandulph, our ſwords ſhall bleſſe our ſelues agen :
Prepare thee *Iohn*, Lords follow me your King. [*Exeunt.*

          I 2.   K. *Iohn.*

K. Iohn. Accurfed *Iohn*, the diuell owes thée ſhame,
Reſiſting *Rome*, or yeelding to the Pope, all's one.
The diuell take the Pope, the Peeres, and *Fraunce* :
Shame be my ſhare for yeelding to the Prieſt.

Pand. Comfort thy ſelfe King *Iohn*, the Cardinall goes
Vpon his curſe to make them leaue their armes. [*Exit.*

Phil. Comfort my Lord, and curſe the Cardinall,
Betake your ſelfe to armes, my troupes are preſt
To anſwer *Lewis* with a luſtie ſhocke :
The *Engliſh* archers haue their quiuers full,
Their bowes are bent, the pikes are preſt to puſh :
Good cheere my Lord, King *Richards* fortune hangs
Vpon the plume of warrelike *Philips* helme.
Then let them know his brother and his ſonne
Are leaders of the *Engliſhmen* at armes.

K. Iohn. Philip I know not how to anſwer thee :
But let us hence, to anſwer *Lewis* pride.

Excurſians. Enter Meloun *with Engliſh Lords.*

Meloun. O I am ſlaine, Nobles, *Saliſbury, Pembroke,*
My ſoule is charged, heare me : for what I ſay
Concerns the Peeres of *England,* and their State.
Liſten, braue Lords, a fearfull mourning tale
To be deliuered by a man of death.
Behold theſe ſcarres, the dole of bloudie *Mars*
Are harbingers from natures common foe,
Citing this truncke to *Tellus* priſon houſe ;
Lifes charter (Lordings) laſteth not an houre :
And fearefull thoughts, forerunners of my end,
Bid me giue phyſicke to a ſickely ſoule.
O Peeres of *England,* know you what you do ?

                                                    There's

There's but a halfe that funders you from harme,
The hooke is baited, and the traine is made,
And fimply you run doating to your deaths.
But left I die, and leaue my tale vntolde,
With filence flaughtering fo braue a crew,
This Patuerre, if *Lewis* winne the day,
There's not an *Englifhman* that lifts his hand
Againft King *Iohn* to plant the heire of *Fraunce*,
But is already damnd to cruell death.
I heard it vow'd ; my felfe amongft the reft
Swore on the Altar aid to this Edict.
Two caufes Lords, make me difplay this drift,
The greateft for the freedome of my foule,
That longs to leaue this manfion free from guilt :
The other on a naturall inftinct,
For that my Grandfire was an *Englifhman.*
Mifdoubt not Lords the truth of my difcourfe,
No frenfie, nor no brainficke idle fit,
But well aduifde, and wotting what I fay,
Pronounce I here before the face of heauen,
That nothing is difcouered but a truth.
Tis time to flie, fubmit your felues to *Iohn*,
The fmiles of *Fraunce* made in the frownes of death,
Lift vp your fwords, turne face againft the *French*,
Expell the yoke that's framed for your necks.
Backe warremen, backe, imbowell not the clime;
Your feate, your nurfe, your birth dayes breathing place,
That bred you, beares you, brought you vp in armes.
Ah! be not fo ingrate to digge your mothers graue,
Preferue your lambes and beate away the wolfe.
My foule hath faid, contritions penitence

I 3   Laies

Laies hold on mans redemption for my sinne.
Farewell my Lords; witnesse my faith when we are met
    in heauen,
And for my kindnesse giue me graue roome here.
My soule doth fleet, worlds vanities farewell.   [*Dies.*

    Salisb. Now ioy betide thy soule well-meaning man,
How now my Lords, what cooling carde is this ?
A greater griefe growes now than earst hath beene.
What counsell giue you, shall we stay and die,
Or shall we home, and kneele vnto the King ?

    Pemb. My heart misgaue this sad accursed newes :
What haue we done ? fie Lords, what frensie moued
Our hearts to yeeld vnto the pride of *Fraunce ?*
If we perseuer, we are sure to die :
If we desist, small hope againe of life.

    Salisb. Beare hence the body of this wretched man,
That made vs wretched with his dying tale,
And stand not wayling on our present harmes,
As women wont : but seeke our harmes redresse.
As for my selfe, I will in haste be gone :
And kneele for pardon to our soueraigne *Iohn.*

    Pemb. I, there's the way, let's rather kneele to him,
Than to the *French* that would confound vs all. [*Exeunt.*

    Enter King Iohn *carried betweene two Lords,*

    K. Iohn. Set downe, set downe the loade not woorth
      your paine,
For done I am with deadly wounding griefe :
Sickely and succourlesse, hopelesse of any good,
The world hath wearied me, and I haue wearied it :
It loathes I liue, I liue and loathe my selfe.

                         Who

Who pities me? to whom haue I been kinde?
But to a few; a few will pity me.
Why die I not? Death scornes so vilde a prey.
Why liue I not? Life hates so sad a prize.
I sue to both to be retaind of either,
But both are deafe, I can be heard of neither.
Nor death nor life, yet life and neare the neere,
Ymixt with death, biding I wot not where.

Phil. How fares my Lord, that he is carried thus?
Not all the aukeward fortunes yet befalne,
Made such impreffion of lament in me.
Nor euer did my eye attaint my heart
With any obiect moouing more remorse,
Than now beholding of a mighty King,
Borne by his Lords in such diftreffed State.

K. Iohn. What newes with thee? if bad, report it
straight;
If good, be mute, it doth but flatter me.

Phil. Such as it is, and heauy though it be,
To glut the world with tragicke elegies,
Once will I breathe to aggrauate the reft,
Another moane to make the meafure full.
The braueft bow-man had not yet fent forth
Two arrowes from the quiuer at his fide,
But that a rumour went throughout our Campe,
That *Iohn* was fled, the King had left the field.
At laft the rumour fcal'd thefe eares of mine,
Who rather chofe a facrifice for *Mars*,
Than ignominious fcandall by retire.
I cheer'd the troupes, as did the Prince of *Troy*,
His weary followers gainft the *Mermidons*,
Crying alowd, S. *George*, the day is ours.

But

But feare had captiuated courage quite,
And like the Lambe before the greedie Wolfe,
So heartlesse fled our warremen from the field.
Short tale to make, my selfe amongst the rest,
Was faine to fly before the eager foe.
By this time night had shadowed all the earth,
With sable curtaines of the blackest hue,
And fenc'd us from the furie of the French,
As Io from the iealous Iunoes eie.
When in the morning our troupes did gather head,
Passing the washes with our carriages,
The impartiall tide deadly and inexorable,
Came raging in with billowes threatning death,
And swallowed vp the most of all our men,
My selfe vpon a Galloway right free, well pac'd,
Out stript the floudes that followed waue by waue,
I so escap'd to tell this tragicke tale.

   K. Iohn. Griefe vpon griefe, yet none so great a griefe
To end this life, and thereby rid my griefe.
Was euer any so infortunate,
The right Idea of a cursed man,
As I, poore I, a triumph for despight?
My feuer growes, what ague shakes me so?
How farre to *Swinstead*, tell me, do you know?
Present vnto the Abbot word of my repaire,
My sicknesse rages, to tyrannike vpon me,
I cannot liue vnlesse this feuer leaue me.

   Phil. Good cheere my Lord, the Abbey is at hand,
Behold my Lord, the Churchmen come to meet you.

         Enter

Enter the Abbot and certaine Monkes.

Abb. All health and happines to our foueraigne Lord
  the King.

K. Iohn. Nor health nor happines hath *Iohn* at all.
Say Abbot, am I welcome to thy houfe?

Abb. Such welcome as our Abbey can afford,
Your maieftie fhall be affured of.

Phil. The King thou feeft is weake and uery faint,
What victuals haft thou to refrefh his Grace?

Abb. Good ftore my Lord, of that you need not feare,
For *Lincolnefhire,* and thefe our Abbey grounds
Were neuer fatter, nor in better plight.

K. Iohn. Philip, thou neuer needft to doubt of cares
Nor King nor Lord is feated halfe fo well,
As are the Abbeis throughout all the land,
If any plot of ground do paffe another,
The friars faften on it ftrait:
But let vs in to tafte of their repaft,
It goes againft my heart to feed with them,
Or be beholding to fuch Abbey groomes.   [*Exeunt.*

Manet a Monke.

Monke. Is this the King that neuer lou'd a Friar?
Is this the man that doth contemne the Pope?
Is this the man that rob'd the holy Church,
And yet will flie vnto a Friary?
Is this the King that aymes at Abbeis lands?
Is this the man whom all the world abhorres,
And yet will flie vnto a Friary?

                              Accurft

Accurst be *Swinstead* Abbey, Abbot, Friars,
Monkes, Nunnes, and Clerks, and all that dwell therein,
If wicked *Iohn* escape aliue away.
Now if that thou wilt looke to merit heauen,
And be canonized for a holy Saint :
To pleafe the world with a deferuing worke,
Be thou the man to fet thy countrey free,
And murder him that feekes to murder thee.

Enter the Abbot.

Abbot. Why are not you within to cheere the King ?
He now begins to mend, and will to meate.
Monke. What if I fay to ftrangle him in his fleepe ?
Abb. What, at thy *Mumpfimus ?* away,
And feeke fome meanes for to paftime the King.
Monke. Ile fet a dudgeon dagger at his heart,
And with a mallet knocke him on the head.
Abb. Alas, what meanes this monke to murder me ?
Dare lay my Life hee'l kill me for my place.
Monke. I'll poyfon him, and it fhall ne'r be knowne,
And then fhall I be chiefeft of my houfe.
Abb. If I were dead indeed he is the next,
But Ile away, for why the Monke is mad,
And in his madneffe he will murder me.
Monke. My Ld. I cry your Lordfhip mercy, I faw you
not.
Abb. Alas good *Thomas* do not murder me, and thou
fhalt haue my place with thoufand thanks.
Monke. I murder you ! God fhield from fuch a thought !
Abb. If thou wilt needs, yet let one fay my prayers.
Monke. I will not hurt your Lordfhip good my Lord :
                                                    but

but if you pleafe, I will impart a thing that fhall be be-
neficiall to vs all.

Abb. Wilt thou not hurt me holy Monke? fay on.

Monke. You know my Lord, the King is in our houfe.

Abb. True.

Monke. You know likewife the King abhorres a Friar.

Abb. True.

Monke. And he that loues not a Friar is our enemy.

Abb. Thou faift true.

Monke. Then the King is our enemy.

Abb. True.

Monke. Why then fhould we not kil our enemy, and
the King being our enemy, why then fhould we not kill
the King.

Abb. O bleffed Monke, I fee God moues thy minde
To free this land from tyrants flauery.
But who dare venter for to do this deede?

Monke. Who dare? why I my Lord dare do the deede,
Ile free my countrey and the Church from foes,
And merit heauen by killing of a King.

Abb. Thomas kneele downe, and if thou art refolu'd,
I will abfolue thee here from all thy finnes,
For why the deede is meritorious.
Forward, and feare not man, for euery month,
Our Friars fhall fing a maffe for *Thomas* foule.

Monke. God and S. *Francis* profper my attempt,
For now my Lord I goe about my worke.   [*Exeunt.*

Enter Lewis *and his armie.*

Lewis. Thus victorie in bloudie lawrell tlad,
Followes the fortune of yong *Ledowike,*

The

The *Englishmen* as danted at our fight,
Fall as the fowle before the Eagles eies,
Onely two croffes of contrary change
Do nip my heart, and vex me with vnreft.
Lord *Melouns* death, the one part of my foule,
A brauer man did neuer liue in *Fraunce.*
The other griefe, I that's a gall indeed,
To thinke that *Douer* caftle fhould hold out
Gainft all affaults, and reft impregnable.
Yee warrelike race of *Francus, Hectors* fonne,
Triumph in conqueft of that tyrant *Iohn,*
The better halfe of *England* is our owne :
And towards the conqueft of the other part,
We haue the face of all the *Englifh* Lords,
What then remaines but ouerrun the land ?
Be refolute my warrelike followers,
And if good fortune ferue as fhe begins,
The pooreft pefant of the realme of *Fraunce*
Shall be a mafter ore an *Englifh* Lord.

Enter a Meffenger.

Lewis. Fellow, what newes ?

Meff. Pleafeth your Grace, the Earle of *Salifbury,*
Pembroke, Effex, Clare, and *Arundell,* with all the Barons
that did fight for thee, are on a fodaine fled with all their
powers, to ioyne with *Iohn,* to driue thee back againe.

Enter another Meffenger.

Meff. Lewis my Lord, why ftandft thou in a maze ?
Gather thy troupes, hope not of helpe from *Fraunce,*
For all thy forces being fifty faile,

Containing

Containing twenty thoufand foldiers,
With victuall and munition for the warre,
Putting them from *Callis* in vnluckie time,
Did croffe the feas, and on the *Goodwin* fands,
The men, munition, and the fhips are loft.

Enter another Meffenger.

 Lewis. More newes ? fay on.
 Meff. *Iohn* (my Lord) with all his fcattered troups,
Flying the fury of your conquering fword,
As *Pharaoh* earft within the bloody fea,
So he and his enuironed with the tide,
On *Lincolne* wafhes all were ouerwhelmed,
The Barons fled, our forces caft away.
 Lewis. Was euer heard fuch vnexpected newes ?
 Meff. Yet *Lodowike* reuiue thy dying heart,
King *Iohn* and all his forces are confumde.
The leffe thou needft the aid of *Englifh* earles,
The leffe thou needft to grieue thy nauies wracke,
And follow times aduantage with fucceffe.
 Lewis, Braue *Frenchmen* arm'd with magnanimitie,
March after *Lewis,* who will lead you on
To chafe the Barons power that wants a head,
For *Iohn* is drown'd, and I am *Englands* King.
Though our munition and our men be loft,
Philip of *Fraunce* will fend vs frefh fupplies. [*Exeunt.*

Enter two Friars laying a Cloth.

 Friar. Difpatch difpatch, the King defires to eate,
Would a might eat his laft for the loue he beares to
 church men.
      K   *Friar.*

Friar. I am of thy mind too, and so it should be and we might be our own caruers.

I maruell why they dine here in the Orchard.

Friar. I know not, nor I care not. The King comes.

K. Iohn. Come on Lord Abbot, shall we sit together?

Abb. Pleaseth your Grace sit downe.

K. Iohn. Take your places, sirs, no pomp in penury, all beggers and friends may come, where Necessitie keeps the house, curtesie is barr'd the table, sit downe *Philip.*

Phil. My Lord, I am loth to allude so much to the prouerb, honors change maners: a king is a king, though fortune do her worst, and we as dutifull in despite of her frown, as if your highnes were now in the highest tipe of dignitie.

K. Iohn. Come, no more adoe, and you tell mee much of dignity, you'l marre my appetite in a surfet of sorrow. What cheere Lord Abbot, me thinks ye frown like an host that knows his guest hath no money to pay the reckning?

Abb. No my liege, if I frowne at all, it is for I feare this cheere too homely to entertaine so mighty a guest as your maiestie.

Phil. I thinke rather, my Lord Abbot, you remember my last being here, when I went in progresse for powches, and the rancour of his heart breakes out in his countenance, to shew he hath not forgot me.

Abb. Not so my Lord, you, and the meanest follower of his maiesty, are heartily welcome to me.

Monke. Wassell my Liege, and as a poore Monke may say, welcome to *Swinstead.*

K. Iohn. Begin Monke, and report hereafter thou wast taster to a King.

Monke.

Monke. As much health to your highneſſe as to mine
owne heart.

K. Iohn. I pledge thee kind Monke.

Monke. The merrieſt draught that euer was drunke in
    England.

Am I not too bold with your Highneſſe?

 -*K. Iohn.* Not a whit, all friends and fellowes for a time.

Monke. If the inwards of a toad be a compound of any
· proofe: why ſo it workes.

K. Iohn. Stay *Philip,* where's the Monke?

Phil. He is dead my Lord.

K. Iohn. Then drinke not *Philip* for a world of wealth.

Phil. What cheere my liege? your collor gins to
    change.

K. Iohn. So doth my life: O *Philip,* I am poiſon'd.

The Monke, the Diuell, the poyſon gins to rage,
It will depoſe my ſelfe a King from raigne.

Phil. This Abbot hath an intereſt in this aſt.

At all aduentures take thou that from me.
There lie the Abbot, Abbey, Lubber, Diuell.
March with the Monke vnto the gates of hell.
How fares my Lord?

K. Iohn. *Philip,* ſome drinke, oh for the frozen Alpes,
To tumble on and coole this inward heate,
That rageth as the fornace ſeuen-fold hot,
To burne the holy three in *Babylon :*
Power after power forſake their proper power,
Only the heart impugnes with faint reſiſt
The fierce inuade of him that conquers Kings.
Helpe God, O paine! die *Iohn,* O plague
Inflicted on thee for thy grieuous ſinnes.
Philip, a chaire, and by and by a graue,

        K 2   **My**

My legges difdaine the carriage of a King.

   Phil. A good my liege, with patience conquer griefe,
And beare this paine with kingly fortitude.

   K. Iohn. Me thinkes I fee a catalogue of finne,
Wrote by a fiende in marble characters,
The leaft enough to loofe my part in heauen.
Me thinkes the Diuell whifpers in mine eares,
And tells me, tis in vaine to hope for grace,
I muft be damn'd for *Arthurs* fodaine death.
I fee, I fee a thoufand thoufand men
Come to accufe me for my wrong on earth,
And there is none fo mercifull a God
That will forgiue the number of my finnes.
How haue I liu'd, but by anothers loffe ?
What haue I lou'd, but wracke of others weale ?
When haue I vow'd, and not infring'd mine oath ?
Where haue I done a deede deferuing well ?
How, what, when, and where, haue I beftow'd a day,
That tended not to fome notorious ill.
My life repleate with rage and tyrannie,
Craues little pittie for fo ftrange a death.
Or, who will fay that *Iohn* deceafde too foone ?
Who will not fay, he rather liu'd too long ?
Difhonour did attaint me in my life,
And fhame attendeth *Iohn* vnto his death.
Why did I fcape the fury of the *French*,
And dide not by the temper of their fwords ?
Shameleffe my life, and fhamefully it ends,
Scorn'd by my foes, difdained of my friends.

   Phil. Forgiue the world and all your earthly foes,
And call on Chrift, who is your lateft friend.

                            K. Iohn

K. Iohn. My tongue doth falter: *Philip*, I tell thee man,
Since *Iohn* did yield vnto the Prieft of *Rome*,
Nor he nor his haue profpred on the earth:
Curft are his bleffings, and his curfe is bliffe.
But in the fpirit I crie vnto my God,
As did the kingly prophet *Dauid* cry,
(Whofe hands, as mine, with murder were attaint)
I am not he fhall build the Lord a houfe,
Or roote thefe locufts from the face of earth:
But if my dying heart deceiue me not,
From out thefe loynes fhall fpring a kingly braunch
Whofe armes fhall reach vnto the gates of *Rome*,
And with his feete treade downe the Strumpets pride,
That fits vpon the chaire of *Babylon*.
Philip, my heart ftrings breake, the poyfons flame
Hath ouercome in me weake Natures power,
And in the faith of Iefu *Iohn* doth die.

   Philip. See how he ftriues for life; vnhappy Lord,
Whofe bowels are diuided in themfelues.
This is the fruit of Poperie, when true kings
Are flaine and fhouldred out by Monkes and Friars.

Enter a Meffenger.

   Meff. Pleafe it your Grace, the Barons of the Land,
Which all this while bare armes againft the King,
Conducted by the Legate of the Pope,
Together with the Prince his Highneffe fonne,
Do craue to be admitted to the prefence of the King.
   Philip. Your Sonne, my Lord, yong *Henry* craues to fee
Your Maieftie, and brings with him befide
The Barons that reuolted from your Grace.

K 3

O piercing

O piercing fight, he fumbleth in the mouth,
His fpeech doth faile : lift vp your felfe my Lord,
And fee the Prince to comfort you in death.

Enter Pandulph, *yong* Henry, *the Barons with daggers in their hands.*

   Prince Henry. O let me fee my father ere he die :
O vncle, were you here, and fuffred him
To be thus poyfned by a damned Monke ?
Ah he is dead, Father, fweet Father fpeake.
   Phil. His fpeach doth faile, he hafteth to his end.
   Pand. Lords, giue me leaue to ioy the dying King,
With fight of thefe his Nobles kneeling here
With daggers in their hands, who offer vp
Their liues for ranfome of their foul offence.
Then good my Lord, if you forgiue them all,
Lift vp your hand in token you forgiue.
   Salifb. We humbly thanke your royall Maieftie,
And vow to fight for *England* and her King :
And in the fight of *Iohn* our foueraigne Lord,
In fpite of *Lewis* and the power of *Fraunce,*
Who hitherward are marching in all hafte,
We crowne yong *Henry* in his fathers fted.
   Prince Henry. Help, help, he dies ; ah father ! looke
   on mee.
   Pand. K. *Iohn,* farewell : in token of thy faith,
And figne thou dieft the feruant of the Lord,
Lift vp thy hand, that we may witneffe here,
Thou diedft the feruant of our Sauiour Chrift.
Now ioy betide thy foule : what noife is this ?

Enter

Enter a Meſſenger.

Meſſ. Help Lords, the Dolphin maketh hitherward
With Enſignes of defiance in the winde,
And all our armie ſtandeth at a gaze,
Expecting what their Leaders will commaund.

Phil. Let's arme our ſelues in yong K. *Henries* right,
And beate the power of *Fraunce* to ſea againe.

Pand. Philip not ſo, but I will to the Prince,
And bring him face to face to parley with you.

Phil. Lord *Saliſbury,* your ſelfe ſhall march with me,
So ſhall we bring theſe troubles to an end.

King Henry. Sweet vncle, if thou loue thy Soueraigne,
Let not a ſtone of *Swinſtead* Abbey ſtand,
But pull the houſe about the Friars eares:
For they haue kill'd my Father and my King. [*Exeunt.*

A Parley ſounded, Lewis, Pandulph, Saliſbury, *&c.*

Pand. Lewis of *Fraunce,* yong *Henry, Englands* King
Requires to know the reaſon of the claime
That thou canſt make to any thing of his.
King *Iohn* that did offend, is dead and gone,
See where his breathleſſe trunke in preſence lies,
And he as heire apparant to the crowne
Is now ſucceeded in his Fathers roome.

Re-enter Henry and the Barons.

King Henry. Lewis, what law of armes doth leade
  thee thus,
To keepe poſſeſſion of my lawfull right?
Anſwere; in fine, if thou wilt take a peace,

And

And make surrender of my right againe,
Or trie thy title with the dint of sword :
I tell thee Dolphin, *Henry* feares thee not.
For now the Barons cleaue vnto their King,
And what thou haft in *England* they did get.

   Lewis. *Henry* of *England*, now that *Iohn* is dead,
That was the chiefeft enemie to *Fraunce*.
I may the rather be inducde to peace.
But *Salisbury*, and you Barons of the Realme,
This ftrange reuolt agrees not with the oath
That you on *Bury* Altare lately fware.

   Salisb. Nor did the oath your Highneffe there did take
Agree with th' honour of the Prince of *Fraunce*,

   Phil. My Lord, what anfwer make you to the King?

   Dolphin. Faith *Philip* this I fay: It bootes not me.
Nor any Prince nor power of *Chriftendome*
To feeke to win this Iland *Albion*,
Vnleffe he haue a partie in the Realme.
By treafon for to help him in his warres.
The Peeres which were the partie on my fide
Are fled from me: then bootes not me to fight,
But on conditions, as mine honour will,
I am contented to depart the Realme.

   K. Henry. On what conditions will your Highnes yeeld?

   Lewis. That fhall we thinke vpon by more aduice.

   Phil. Then Kings and Princes, let thefe broils haue end,
And at more leifure talke vpon the League.
Meane while to *Worfter* let vs beare the King,
And there interre his bodie, as befeemes,
But firft, in fight of *Lewis* heire of *Fraunce*,
Lords take the Crowne, and fet it on his head,
That by fucceffion is our lawfull King.

                      They.

They crowne yong Henry.

Thus *Englands* peace begins in *Henries* raigne,
And bloodie warres are clofde with happie league.
Let *England* liue but true within itfelfe,
And all the world can neuer wrong her State:
Lewis, thou fhalt be brauely fhipt to *Fraunce,*
For neuer *Frenchman* got of *Englifh* ground
The twentieth part that thou haft conquered.
Dolphin, thy hand; to *Worfter* we will march:
Lords all, lay hands to beare your Soueraigne
With obfequies of honour to his graue:
If *Englands* Peeres and people ioyne in one,
Nor Pope, nor *Fraunce,* nor *Spaine* can do them wrong.

THE
METAMORPHOSIS
OF
PIGMALIONS IMAGE.
AND
Certaine SATYRES.

By IOHN MARSTON.

AT LONDON,
Printed for Edmond Matts; and are
to be fold at the figne of the hand and
Plough in Fleetftreete.
1598.
Reprinted 1764.

TO THE

WORLDS

MIGHTIE MONARCH,

GOOD OPINION:

Sole Regent of Affection, perpetuall Ruler
of Iudgement, moſt famous Iuſtice of Cen-
ſures, only giuer of Honor, great procurer
of Aduancement, the Worlds chiefe Ballance, the All of all, and All in all, by
whom all things are yet that they are. I
humbly offer thys my Poem.

*T*Hou *foule of Pleaſure, Honors only ſubſtance,*
   Great Arbitrator, Umpire of the Earth,
Whom fleſhly Epicures call Vertues eſſence,
Thou moouing Orator, whoſe powrefull breath
   Swaies all mens iudgements. Great OPINION,
   Vouchſafe to guild my imperfection.

           L   If

If thou but daine to grace my blushing stile,
And crowne my Muse with good opinion:
If thou vouchsafe with gracious eye to smile
Vpon my young new-born Inuention,
   Ile sing an Hymne in honour of thy name,
   And add some Trophie to enlarge thy fame.

But if thou wilt not with thy Deitie
Shade, and inmaske the errors of my pen,
Protect an Orphane Poets infancie,
I will disclose, that all the world shall ken
   How partiall thou art in Honors giuing:
   Crowning the shade, the substance praise de-
     priuing.

                           W. K.

THE

THE
ARGUMENT
Of the POEM.

*P*IGMALION whofe chaft mind all the
 beauties in Cyprus could not enfnare, yet
at the length hauing carued in Iuorie an ex-
cellent proportion of a beauteous woman, was
fo deeplie enamored on his owne workmanfhip, that he would oftentimes lay the Image
in bedde with him, and fondlie vfe fuch pe-
titions and dalliance, as if it had been a breathing creature. But in the end, finding his
fond dotage, and yet perfeuering in his ardent
affection, made his deuout prayers to *Venus*,
that fhe would vouchfafe to enfpire life into
his Loue, and then ioyne them both toge-

L 2   ther

ther in marriage. Whereupon *Venus* gra-
ciously condiscending to his earnest sute, the
Mayde, (by the power of her Deitie) was
metamorphosed into a liuing Woman. And
After, *Pigmalion* (beeing in Cyprus,) begat
a sonne of her, which was called *Paphus*;
whereupon, that Iland Cyprus, in honor of
Venus, was after, and is now, called by the
inhabitants, *Paphos*.

To his

To his MISTRES.

MY wanton Muſe laſciuiouſly doth ſing
    Of ſportiue loue, of louely dallying.
O beauteous Angell, daine thou to infuſe
A ſprightly wit, into my dulled Muſe.
I inuocate none other Saint but thee,
To grace the firſt bloomes of my Poeſie.
Thy fauours like Promethean *ſacred fire,*
In dead, and dull conceit can life inſpire.
Or like that rare and rich Elixar ſtone,
Can turn to gold, leaden inuention:
Be gracious th.n, and daine to ſhow in mee,
The mighty power of thy Deitie.
And as thou read'ſt, (Faire) take compaſſion,
Force me not enuie my Pigmalion.
   Then when thy kindnes grants me ſuch ſweet
      bliſſe,
Ee gladly write thy metamorphoſis.

PIGMALION.

I.

*P*IGMALION, whofe kie loue-hating minde
  Difdain'd to yeeld feruile affection,
Or amorous fate to any woman-kinde,
Knowing their wants, and mens perfection.
  Yet loue at length fore'd him to know his fate,
  And loue the fhade, whofe fubftance he did hate.

II.

For hauing wrought in pureft Iuorie,
So faire an Image of a Woman's feature,
That neuer yet proudeft mortalitie
Could fhow fo rare and beautious a creature.
  (Vnleffe my Miftres all-excelling face,
  Which giues to heautie, beauties onely grace.)

III.

He was amazed at the wondrous rareneffe
Of his owne workmanfhips perfection.

He

He thought that Nature nere produc'd such fairenes
In which all beauties haue their mantion.
  And thus admiring, was enamored
  On that fayre Image himselfe portraied.

IV.

And naked as it stood before his eyes,
Imperious Loue declares his Deitie.
O what alluring beauties he descries
In each part of his faire imagery!
  Her nakednes, each beauteous shape containes ;
  All beautie in her nakednes remaines.

V.

He thought he saw the blood run through the vaine:
And leape, and swell with all alluring meanes ;
Then feares he is deceiu'd, and then againe,
He thinkes he see'th the brightnes of the beames
  Which shoote from out the fairenes of her eye :
  At which he stands as in an extasie.

VI.

Her amber-coloured, her shining haire,
Makes him protest, the Sunne hath spread her head
With golden beames, to make her farre more faire.
But when her cheeks his amorous thoughts haue fed,
  Then he exclaimes, such redde and so pure white,
  Did neuer blesse the eye of mortal sight.

Then

VII.

Then view's her lips, no lips did seeme so faire
In his conceit, through which he thinks doth flie
So sweet a breath, that doth perfume the ayre.
Then next her dimpled chin he doth discry,
   And views, and wonders, and yet views her still.
   " Loues eyes in viewing neuer haue their fill."

VIII.

Her breasts, like polisht Iuory appeare,
Whose modest mount, doe blesse admiring eye,
And makes him wish for such a Pillowbeare.
Thus fond *Pigmalion* striueth to discry
   Each beauteous part, not letting ouer-slip
   One parcell of his curious workmanship.

IX.

Vntill his eye distended so farre downe
That it discried Loues pauillion :
Where *Cupid* doth enioy his onely crowne,
And *Venus* hath her chiefest mansion :
   There would he winke, and winking looke againe,
   Both eyes and thoughts would gladly there remaine.

X.

Who euer saw the subtile Citty-dame
In sacred church, when her pure thoughts shold pray,
Peire

Peire through her fingers, so to hide her shame,
When that her eye, her mind would faine bewray.
  So would he view, and winke, and view againe,
  A chaster thought could not his eyes retaine.

XI.

He wondred that she blusht not when his eye
Saluted those same parts of secrecie :
Conceiting not it was imagerie
That kindly yeelded that large libertie.
  O that my Mistres were an Image too,
  That I might blameles her perfections view.

XII.

But when the faire proportion of her thigh
Began appeare. O *Ouid* would he cry,
Did ere *Corinna* show such Iuorie
When she appeared in *Venus* liuorie ?
  And thus enamour'd dotes on his owne Art
  Which he did work, to work his pleasing smart.

XIII.

And fondly doting, oft he kist her lip :
Oft would he dally with her Iuory breasts.
No wanton loue-trick would he ouer-slip,
But still obseru'd all amorous beheasts.
  Whereby he thought he might procure the loue
  Of his dull Image, which no plaints coulde moue.

                        | Looke

XIV.

Looke how the peeuiſh Papiſts crouch and kneele,
To ſome dum Idoll with their offering,
As if a ſenceleſs carued ſtone could feele
The ardor of his bootles chattering :
    So fond he was, and earneſt in his ſute
    To his remorſles Image, dum and mute.

XV.

He oft doth wiſh his ſoule might part in ſunder
So that one halfe in her had reſidence :
Oft he exclaimes, O beauties onely wonder !
Sweet modell of delight, faire excellence,
    Be gracious vnto him that formed thee,
    Compaſſionate his true-loues ardencie.

XVI.

She with her ſilence ſeemes to graunt his ſute.
Then he all iocund like a wanton louer,
With amorous embracements doth ſalute
Her ſlender waſt, preſuming to diſcouer
    The vale of Loue, where *Cupid* doth delight
    To ſport, and dally all the ſable night.

XVII.

His eyes, her eyes, kindly encountered,
His breaſt, her breaſt, oft ioyned cloſe vnto,
His armes embracements oft ſhe ſuffered,
Hands, armes, eyes, tongue, lips, and all parts did woe.
    His thigh, with hers, his knee playd with her knee,
    A happy conſort when all parts agree.

                          But

XVIII.

But when he faw poor foule he was deceaued,
(Yet, fcarce he could beleeue his fence had failed)
Yet when he found all hope from him bereaued,
And faw how fondly all his thoughts had erred,
   Then did he like to poor *Ixiom* feeme,
   That clipt a cloud in fteede of heauens Queene.

XIX.

I oft haue fmil'd to fee the foolery
Of fome fweet Youths, who ferioufly proteft
That loue refpects not actual Luxury,
But onely ioys to dally, fport, and ieft :
   Loue is a child, contented with a toy,
   A bufk-point, or fome fauour ftill's the boy.

XX.

Marke my *Pigmalion*, whofe affections ardor
May be a mirror to pofteritie.
Yet viewing, touching, kiffing, (common fauour)
Could neuer fatiat his loues ardencie :
   And therefore Ladies, thinke that they more loue you,
   Who do not vnto more than kiffing moue you.

XXI.

For *Pigmalion* kift, viewd, and imbraced,
And yet exclaimes, why were thefe women made
O facred Gods! and with fuch beauties graced ?
Haue they not power as well to coole, and fhade,
   As for to heate mens harts ? or is there none
   Or are they all like mine ? relentleffe ftone.

                                          With

XXII.

With that he takes her in his louing armes,
And downe within a Downe-bed foftly layd her,
Then on his knees he all his fences charmes,
To inuocate fweet *Venus* for to raife her
    To wifhed life, and to infufe fome breath,
    To that which dead, yet gaue a life to death.

XXIII.

Thou facred Queene of fportiue dallying,
(Thus he begins) Loues onely Empereffe,
Whofe kingdome refts in wanton reuelling,
Let me befeech thee fhew thy powerfullneffe
    In changing ftone to flefh, make her relent,
    And kindly yeeld to thy fweet blandifhment.

XXIV.

O gracious Gods, take compaffion.
Inftill into her fome celeftiall fire,
That fhe may equalize affection,
And haue a mutuall loue, and loues defire.
    Thou know'ft the force of loue, then pitty me,
    Compaffionate my true loues ardencie.

XXV.

Thus hauing faid, he rifeth from the floore,
As if his foule diuined him good fortune,

M   Hoping

Hoping his prayers to pitty moou'd fome power.
For all his thoughts did all good luck importune.
   And therefore ftraight he ftrips him naked quite,
   That in the bedde he might haue more delight.

XXVI.

Then thus, Sweet fheetes he fayes, which nowe do couer,
The Idol of my foule, the faireft one
That ever lou'd, or had an amorous louer.
Earths onely modell of perfection,
   Sweet happy fheetes, daine for to take me in,
   That I my hopes and longing thoughts may win.

XXVII.

With that his nimble limbs doe kiffe the fheetes,
And now he bowes him for to lay him downe,
And now each part, with her faire parts doe meet,
Now doth he hope for to enioy loues crowne:
   Now do they dally, kiffe, embrace together,
   Like *Leda's* Twins at fight of faireft weather.

XXVIII.

Yet all's conceit. But fhadow of that bliffe
Which now my Mufe ftriues fweetly to difplay
In this my wondrous metamorphofis.
Daine to beleeve me, now I fadly fay,
   The ftonie fubftance of his Image feature,
   Was ftraight transform'd into a liuing creature.

XXIX.

For when his hands her faire form'd limbs had felt,
And that his armes her naked waist imbraced,
Each part like wax before the sun did melt,
And now, oh now, he finds how he is graced
  By his owne worke.   Tut, women will relent
  When as they finde such mouing blandishment.

XXX.

Doe but conceiue a Mothers passing gladnes,
(After that death her onely sonne had seazed
And ouerwhelm'd her soule with endlesse sadnes)
When that she sees him gin for to be raised
  From out his deadly swoune to life againe:
  Such ioy *Pigmalion* feeles in euery vaine.

XXXI.

And yet he feares he doth but dreaming find
So rich content, and such celestiall blisse.
Yet when he proues and finds her wondrous kind,
Yeelding soft touch for touch, sweet kisse, for kisse,
  He's well assur'd no faire imagery
  Could yeeld such pleasing, loues felicity.

XXXII.

O wonder not to heare me thus relate,
And say to flesh transformed was a stone.

M 2

Had

Had I my Loue in such a wished state
As was afforded to *Pigmalion*,
 Though flinty hard, of her you soone should see
 As strange a transformation wrought by mee.

XXXIII.

And now me thinkes some wanton itching eare
With lustfull thoughts, and ill attention,
Lift's to my Muse, expecting for to heare
The amorous description of that action
 Which *Venus* seekes, and ever doth require,
 When fitnes graunts a place to please desire.

XXXIV.

Let him conceit but what himselfe would doe
When that he obtayned such a fauour,
Of her to whom his thoughts were bound vnto,
If she, in recompence of his loues labour,
 Would daine to let one payre of sheets containe
 The willing bodies of those louing twaine.

XXXV.

Could he, oh could he, when that each to eyther
Did yeeld kind kissing, and more kind embracing,
Could he when that they felt, and clip't together
And might enioy the life of dallying,
 Could he abstaine mid'st such a wanton sporting
 From doing that, which is not fit reporting?

What

XXXVI.

What would he doe when that her softeſt ſkin
Saluted his with a delightfull kiſſe?
When all things fit for loues ſweet pleaſuring
Inuited him to reape a Louers bliſſe?
   What he would doe, the ſelfe ſame action
   Was not neglected by *Pigmalion.*

XXXVII.

For when he found that life had tooke his ſeate
Within the breaſt of his kind beauteous loue,
When that he found that warmth, and wiſhed heate
Which might a Saint and coldeſt ſpirit moue,
   Then arms, eyes, hands, tong, lips, and wanton thigh,
   Were willing agents in Loues luxuris.

XXXVIII.

Who knowes not what enſues? O pardon me,
Yee gaping ears that ſwallow vp my lines
Expect no more. Peace idle Poeſie,
Be not obſceane though wanton in thy rimes.
   And chaſter thoughts, pardon if I doe trip,
   Or if ſome looſe lines from my pen do ſlip.

XXXIX.

Let this ſuffice, that that ſame happy night
So gracious were the Gods of marriage

Mid'ſt

Mid'st all there pleasing and long wish'd delight
Paphus was got: of whom in after age
    Cyprus was *Paphos* call'd, and euermore
    Those Ilandars do *Venus* name adore.

The.

The AUTHOR in prayse of his precedent Poem.

NOW *Rufus*, by old *Glebrons* fearfull mace
Hath not my Muse deseru'd a worthy place?
Come come *Luxurio*, crowne my head with Bayes,
Which like a Paphian, wantonly displayes
The Salaminian titilations,
Which tickle vp our leud Priapians.
Is not my pen compleate? are not my lines
Right in the swaggering humour of these times?
O sing *Peana* to my learned, Muse,
Io bis dicite. Wilt thou refuse?
Doe not I put my Mistres in before?
And pitiously her gracious ayde implore?
Doe not I flatter, call her wondrous faire?
Vertuous, diuine most debonaire?
Hath not my Goddesse in the vaunt-gard place,
The leading of my lines theyr plumes to grace?
And then ensues my stanzaes, like odd bands
Of voluntaries, and mercenarians:
Which like Soldados of our warlike age,
March rich bedight in warlike equipage:
Glittering in dawbed lac'd accoustrements,
And pleasing sutes of loues habiliments.
Yet puffie as Dutch hose they are within,
Faint, and white liuer'd, as our gallants bin:

Patch'd

Patch'd like a beggars cloake, and run as sweet
As doth a tumbrell in the paued street.
And in the end, (the end of loue I wot)
Pigmalion hath a iolly boy begot.
So *Labeo* did complaine his loue was stone,
Obdurate, flinty, so relentlesse none:
Yet *Lynceus* knowes, that in the end of this,
He wrought as strange a metamorphosis.
Ends not my Poem then surpassing ill?
Come, come, *Augustus*, crowne my laureat quill.
    Now by the whyps of *Epigramatists*,
Ile not be lasht for my dissembling shifts.
And therefore I vse Popelings discipline,
Lay ope my faults to *Mastigophoros* eyne:
Censure my selfe, fore others me deride
And scoffe at mee, as if I had deni'd
Or thought my Poem good, when that I see
My lines are froth, my stanzaes saplesse be.
Thus hauing rail'd against my selfe a while,
Ile snarle at those, which doe the world beguile
With masked showes. Ye changing *Proteans* list,
And tremble at a barking Satyrist.

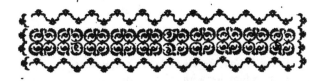

SATYRES.

SATYRE I.

Quedam videntur, & non sunt.

I Cannot show in strange proportion,
Changing my hew like a Camelion.
But you all-canning wits, hold water out,
Yee vizarded-bifronted-*Ianian* rout.
Tell mee browne *Ruscus*, hast thou *Gyges* ring,
That thou presum'st as if thou wert vnseene?
If not. Why in thy wits halfe capreall
Lett'st thou a superscribed Letter fall?
And from thy selfe, vnto thy selfe doost send,
And in the same, thy selfe, thy selfe commend?
For shame leaue running to some *Satrapas*,
Leaue glauering on him in the peopled presse:
Holding him on as he through Paul's doth walke,
With nodds and leggs, and odde superfluous talke:
Making men thinke thee gracious in his sight,
When he esteemes thee but a Parasite.

For

For shame vnmaske, leaue for to cloke intent,
And show thou art vaine-glorious, impudent.
   Come *Briscus*, by the soule of Complement,
I'le not endure that with thine instrument
(Thy Gambo violl plac'd betwixt thy thighes,
Wherein the best part of thy courtship lyes)
Thou entertaine the time, thy Mistres by:
Come, now let's heare thy mounting *Mercurie*,
What mum? Giue him his fiddle once againe,
Or he's more mute then a *Pythagoran*.
But oh! The absolute *Castilie*,
He that can all the poynts of courtship show.
He that can trot a Courser, breake a rush,
And arm'd in proofe, dare dure a strawes strong push.
He, who on his glorious scutchion
Can quaintly show wits newe inuention,
Aduauncing forth some thirstie *Tantalus*,
Or els the Vulture on *Prometheus*,
With some short motto of a dozen lines.
He that can purpose it in dainty rimes,
Can set his face, and with his eye can speake,
Can dally with his Mistres dangling feake,
And wish that he were it, to kisse her eye
And flare about her beauties doitie.
Tut, he is famous for his reuelling,
For fine sette speeches, and for sonetting;
He scornes the violl and the scraping sticke,
And yet's but Broker of anothers wit.
Certes if all things were well knowne and view'd
He doth but champe that which another chew'd.
Come come *Castilio*, skim thy posset curd,
Show thy queere substance, worthlesse, most absurd.
Take

Take ceremonius complement from thee,
Alas, I fee *Caftilios* beggery.
 O if *Democritus* were now aliue
How he would laugh to fee this deuill thriue!
And by an holy femblance bleare mens eyes
When he intends fome damned villanies.
-*Ixion* makes faire weather vnto *Ioue*,
 That he might make foule worke with his faire loue,
And is right fober in his outward femblance,
Demure, and modeft in his countenance;
Applies himfelfe to great *Saturnus* fonne,
Till *Saturns* daughter yeeldes his motion.
Night-fhining *Phœbe* knowes what was begat,
A monftrous Centaure, illegitimate.
 Who would not chuck to fee fuch pleafing fport?
To fee fuch troupes of gallants ftill refort
Vnto *Cornutos* fhop? What other caufe
But chaft *Brownetta*, *Spero* thether drawes?
Who now fo long hath prays'd the Choughs white bill
That he hath left her ne'er a flying quill:
His meaning gain, though outward femblance loue,
So like a Crabfifh *Spero* ftill doth moue.
Laugh, laugh, to fee the world *Democritus*
Cry like that ftrange transformed *Tyreus*.
Now *Sorbo* with a fayned grauity
Doth fifh for honour, and high dignity.
Nothing within, nor yet without, but beard
Which thrice he ftrokes, before I ever heard
One wife graue word, to bleffe my liftning eare.
But marke how Good-opinion doth him reare,
See, he's in office, on his foot-cloth placed:
Now each man caps, and ftriues for to be graced

With

With fome rude nod of his maieftick head,
Which all do wifh in *Limbo* harried.
But O I greeue, that good men daine to be
Slaues unto him, that's flaue to villany.
Now *Sorbo* fwels with felfe conceited fence,
Thinking that men do yeeld this reuerence
Vnto his vertues: fond credulity!
Affe, talke of Ifis, *no man honours thee.*

   Great *Tubrios* feather gallantly doth waue,
Full twenty falls doth make him wondrous braue.
Oh golden Ierkin! Royall arming coate!
Like fhip on Sea, he on the land doth flote.
He's gone, he's fhipt, his refolution
Pricks (by heauen) to this action.
The poxe it doth: not long fince I did view
The man betake him to a common ftew.
And there (I wis) like no quaint ftomack't man
Eates vp his armes. And warres munition
His wauing plume, falls in the Brokers cheft.
Fie that his Oftridge ftomack fhould digeft
His Oftridge feather: eate vp Venis-lace.
Thou that did'ft feare to eate *Poore-Iohns* a fpace.
Lie clofe ye flaue at beaftly luxury!
Melt and confume in pleafures furquedry.
But now, thou that did'ft march with Spanifh Pike before,
Come with French-pox out of that brothell dore.
The fleet's return'd. What news from *Rodio?*
Hote feruice, by the Lord, cries Tubrio.
Why do'ft thou halt? *Why fix times throgh each thigh*
Pufht with the Pike of the hote enemie.
Hote feruice, hote, the Spaniard is a man,
I fay no more, and as a Gentleman

I ferued

I serued in his face. Farwell. Adew.
Welcome from Netherland, from ftreaming ftew,
Affe to thy crib, doffe that huge Lyons fkin,
'Or els the Owle will hoote and driue thee in.
For fhame, for fhame, lew'd liuing *Fabrio*
Prefume not troupe among that gallant crue
Of true Heroike fpirits, come vncafe,
Show vs the true forme of *Dametas* face.
Hence, hence ye flaue, diffemble not thy ftate
But hence-forth be a turne-coate, runnagate.
Oh hold my fides, that I may breake my fpleene,
With laughter at the fhadowes I haue feene.
    Yet I can beare with *Curios* nimble feete
Saluting me with capers in the ftreete,
Although in open view, and peoples face,
He fronts me with fome fpruce, neat, finquepace.
Or *Tullus,* though when ere he me efpies
Straight with loud mouth *(a bandy Sir)* he cries,
Or *Robrus,* who adic't to nimble fence,
Still greetes me with Stockadoes violence.
Thefe I doe beare, becaufe I too well know
They are the fame, they feeme in outward fhow,
But all confufion feuer from mine eye
This Ianian-bifront hypocrifie.

✿✿✿✿✿✿✿✿✿✿✿✿✿✿✿✿✿✿✿✿✿✿✿

SATYRE II.

Quædam funt, & non videntur.

I That euen now lifp'd like an Amorift,
Am turn'd into a fnaphaunce Satyrift.
O tytle, which my iudgement doth adore!
But I dull-fprighted fat Boetian Boore,
Doe farre off honour that Cenforian feate.
But if I could in milk-white robes intreate
Plebieans favour, I would fhew to be
Tribunus plebis, gainft the villany
Of thofe fame *Proteans*, whofe hipocrifie,
Doth ftill abufe our fond credulity.
But finee my felfe am not imaculate,
But many fpots my minde doth vitiate,
I'le leaue the white roabe, and the biting rimes
Vnto our moderne Satyres fharpeft lines;
Whofe hungry fangs fnarle at fome fecret finne.
And in fuch pitchy clouds enwrapped beene
His *Sphinxian* ridles, that old *Oedipus*
Would be amaz'd and take it in foule fnufs
That fuch *Cymerian* darknes fhould inuolue
A quaint conceit, that he could not refolue.
O darknes palpable! Egipts black night!
My wit is ftricken blind, hath loft his fight.
My fhins are broke, with groping for fome fence
To know to what his words haue reference.

Certes

Certes *(funt)* but *(non videntur)* that I know.
Reach me fome Poets Index that will fhow.
Imagines Deorum. Booke of Epithites,
Natales Comes, thou I know recites,
And mak'ft Anatomie of Poefie..
Helpe to unmafke the Satyres fecrefie.
Delphick *Apollo,* ayde me to vnrip,
Thefe intricate deepe Oracles of wit.
Thefe darke Enigmaes, and ftrange ridling fence
Which paffe my dullard braines intelligence.
Fie on my fenceles pate; Now I can fhow
Thou writeft that which I, nor thou, doo'ft know.
Who would imagine that fuch fquint-ey'd fight
Could ftrike the worlds deformities fo right.
But take heede *Pallas,* leaft thou ayme awry
Loue, nor yet Hate, had ere true iudging eye.
Who would once dreame that that fame Elegie,
That faire fram'd peece of fweeteft Poefie,
Which *Muto* put betwixt his Miftris paps,
(When he (quick-witted) call'd her *Cruell Chaps,*
And told her, there fhe might his dolors read
Which fhe, oh fhe, vpon his hart had fpread)
Was penn'd by *Rofcio* the Tragedian?
Yet *Muto,* like a good *Vulcanian,*
An honeft Cuckold, calls the baftard fonne,
And brags of that which others for him done.
Satyre thou lyeft, for that fame Elegie
Is Mutos *owne, his owne deere Poefie:*
Why tis his owne; and deare, for he did pay
Ten crownes for it, as I heard *Rofcius* fay.
Who would imagine yonder fober man,
That fame deuout meale-mouth'd Precifean,

That

That cries *good brother*, *kind sister*, makes a duck,
After the Antique grace, can alwayes pluck
A sacred booke, out of his ciuill hose,
And at th'op'ning, and at our stomacks close
Sayes with a turn'd-vp eye a solemne grace
Of halfe an houre, then with silken face
Smiles on the holy crue, and then doth cry.
O manners! O times of impurity!
With that depaints a church reformed state,
The which the female tongues magnificate;
Because that *Platoes* odd opinion,
Of all things *(common)* hath strong motion
In their weake minds. Who thinks that this good man
Is a vile, sober, damn'd, Polititian?
Not I, till with his baite of purity
He bit me sore in deepest vsury.
No Iew, no Turke, woulde vse a Christian
So inhumanely as this Puritan.
Diomedes Iades were not so bestiall,
As this same seeming-saint, vile Canniball.
Take heede O world, take heede aduisedly
Of these same damned Anthropophagy.
I had rather be within a Harpies clawes
Then trust my selfe in their deuouring iawes.
Who all confusion to the world would bring
Vnder the forme of their new discipline.
O I could say, *Briareus* hundred hands
Were not so ready to bring *Ioue* in bands
As these to set endles contentious strife
Betwixt *Iehoua*, and his sacred wife.
    But see who's yonder, true Humility
The perfect image of faire Curtisie.

See

See, he doth daine to be in feruitude
Where he hath no promotions liuelihood.
Marke, he doth curtfie, and falutes a block,
Will feeme to wonder at a weathercock,
Trenchmore with Apes, play mufick to an Owle,
Bleffe his fweet honours running brafell bowle:
Cries *(brauly brouke)* when that his Lordfhip mift,
And is of all the thrunged fcaffold hift:
O is not this a curteous minded man?
No foole, no, a damn'd Machenelian:
Holds candle to the deuill for a while,
That he the better may the world beguile
That's fed with fhows, He hopes thogh fom repine,
When funne is fet, the leffer ftarres will fhine:
He is within a haughty malecontent,
Though he doe ufe fuch humble blandifhment.
But bold-fac'd Satyre, ftraine not ouer hie,
But laugh and chuck at meaner gullery.

In fayth yon is a well fac'd Gentleman,
See how he paceth like a Ciprian:
Faire Amber treffes of the faireft haire
That ere were waued by our London aire,
Rich laced fuit, all fpruce, all neat in truth.
Ho *Linceus!* What's yonder brifk neat youth
Bout whom yon troupe of Gallants flocken fo?
And now together to *Brownes* common goe?
Thou knowft I'am fure, for thou canft caft thine eio
Through nine mud wals, or els old Poets lie.
Tis loofe legd Lais, *that fame common Drab,*
For whom good Tubrio *tooke the mortall ftab.*
Ha ha, Nay then I'le neuer raile at thofe
That weare a codpis, thereby to difclofe:

What

What sexe they are, since strumpets breeches vse,
And all mens eyes saue *Linceus* can abuse.
Nay steed of shadow, lay the substance out,
Or els fair *Briseus* I shall stand in doubt
What sex thou art, since such Hermaphrodites
Such *Protean* shadowes so delude our sights.
    Looke, looke, with what a discontented grace
Bruto the trauailer doth sadly pace
Long Westminster, O civil seeming shade,
Marke his sad colours, how demurely clad,
Staidnes it selfe, and *Nestors* grauity
Are but the shade of his ciuility.
And now he sighes.   O *thou corrupted age*,
Which slight regard'st men of sound carriage,
Vertue, knowledge, flie to heauen againe,
Daine not mong these vngrateful sots remaine.
Well, some tongs I know, some countries I haue seene
And yet these oily Snailes respectles beene
Of my good parts. O worthles puffie slaue!
Didst thou to *Venis* goe oft els to haue,
But buy a Lute and vse a Curtezan?
And there to liue like a Cyllenian?
And now from thence what hether do'st thou bring?
But surphulings, new paints and poysoning,
Aretines pictures, some strange, Luxury,
And new found vse of *Venis* venery?
What art thou but black clothes? Say *Bruto* say
Art any thing but only say array?
Which I am sure is all thou brought'st from France,
Saue Naples poxe, and French-mens dalliance.
From haughty Spayne, what brought'st thou els beside,
But lofty lookes, and their Lucifrian pride?

                                    From

From Belgia what? but their deep bezeling,
Their boote-carouse, and their Beere-buttering:
Well, then exclaime not on our age good man,
But hence poluted Neopolitan:

    Now Satyre cease to rub our gauled skinnes,
And to vnmaske the worlds detested sinnes.
Thou shalt as soone draw *Nilus* riuer dry,
As cleanse the world from foule impietie.

❊❊❊❊❊❊❊❊ ❊❊❊❊❊❊❊❊

SATYRE III.

Quedam & sunt, & videntur.

NOW grim *Reproofe* swell in my rough-hew'd rime,
   That thou maist vexe the guilty of our time.
Yon is a youth, whom how can I ore slip,
Since he so iumpe doth in my mashes hit?
He hath been longer in preparing him
Then *Terence* wench, and now behold he's seene.
Now after two yeeres fast and earnest prayer,
The fashion change not, (lest he should dispaire
Of euer hoording vp more faire gay clothes)
Behold at length in London streets he showes.
His ruffe did eate more time in neatest setting
Then *Woodstocks* worke in painfull perfecting.
It hath more doubles farre, then *Aiax* shield
When he gainst Troy did furious battle weild.
Nay he doth weare an Embleme bout his neck,
For under that fayre Ruffe so sprucely set

                  Appeares

Appeares a fall, a falling-band forsooth.
O dapper, rare, compleat, sweet nittie youth!
Iesu Maria! How his clothes appeare
Croft and recroft with lace, sure for some feare,
Leaft that some spirit with a tippet Mace
Should with a gaftly show affright his face.
His hat, himselfe, small crowne and huge great brim,.
Faire outward show, and little wit within.
And all the band with feathers he doth fill,
Which is a signe of a fantaftick ftill,
As sure, as (some doe tell me) euermore
A Goate doth ftand before a brothell dore.
His clothes perfum'd, his fustie mouth is ayred,
His chinne new swept, his very cheekes are glazed..

But ho, what *Ganimede* is that doth grace.
The gallants heeles.   One, *who for two daies space*
Is clofely hyred. Now who dares not call
This *Æfops* crow, fond, mad, fantasticall.
Why so he is, his clothes doe sympathize,
And with his inward spirit humorize.
An open Affe, that is not yet so wise
As his derided fondnes to disguise.
Why thou art Bedlam mad, starke lunaticke,
And glori'ft to be counted a fantaftick.
Thou neyther art, nor yet will seeme to be
Heire to some vertuous praised qualitie.
O frantick men! that thinke all villanie
The complete honors of Nobilitie.
When some damn'd vice, some strange mishapen sute,
Make youths esteeme themselues in hie repute.
O age! in which our gallants boaft to be
Slaues vnto riot, and rude luxury!

Nay,

Nay, when they blush, and thinke an honest act
Dooth their supposed vertues maculate l
Bedlame, Frenzie, Madnes, Lunacie,
I challenge all your moody Empery
Once to produce a more distracted man
Then is inamorato *Lucian*.
For when my eares receau'd a fearefull sound
That he was sicke, I went, and there I found
Him layde of loue, and newly brought to bed
Of monstrous folly, and a franticke head.
His chamber hang'd about with Elegies,
With sad complaints of his louers miseries:
His windows strow'd with Sonnets, and the glasse
Drawne full of loue-knots. I approacht the Asse,
And straight he weepes, and sighes some sonnet out
To his faire loue I. And then he goes about
For to perfume her rare perfection
With some sweet-smelling pincke Epitheton.
Then with a melting looke he writhes his head,
And straight in passion riseth in his bed;
And hauing kist his hand, stroke up his haire,
Made a French conge, cryes, O *cruell feare*
To the antique Bed-post. I laught a maine
That down my cheeks the mirthfull drops did raine.
Well hee's no *Ianus*, but substantiall,
In show, and essence a good naturall.
When as thou hear'st me aske spruce *Ducus*
From whence he comes. And he straight answers vs,
From Lady *Lille*. And is going straight
To the Countesse of ( ) for she doth waite
His comming. And will surely send her Coach,
Vnlesse he make the speedier approach.

Art

Art not thou ready for to breake thy spleene
At laughing at the fondnefs thou haft feene
In this vaine-glorious foole ? When thou doft know
He neuer durft vnto thefe Ladies show
His pippin face. Well, he's no accident,
But reall, reall, shamelesse, impudent.
And yet he boafts, and wonders that each man .
Can call him by his name, fweet *Duceus* :
And is right pproude that thus his name is knowne.
I *Duceus*, I, thy name is too farre blowne.
The world too much, thy felfe too little know'ft
Thy priuate felfe. Why then should *Duceus* boaft ?
But humble Satyre, wilt thou daine difplay
Thefe open naggs, which purblind eyes bewray ?
Come, come, and fnarle more darke at fecrete fin,
Which in fuch Laborinths enwrapped him,
That *Ariadne* I muft craue thy ayde
To helpe me finde where this foul monster's layd,
Then will I driue the Minotaure from vs,
And feeme to be a fecond *Thefeus*.

✻✻✻✻✻✻✻✻✻✻✻✻✻✻✻✻✻✻✻✻✻✻✻✻✻

S A T Y R E IV.
R E A C T I O.

NOW doth *Ramnufia Adraftian*,
    Daughter of Night, and of the Ocean
Prouoke my pen. What cold *Saturnian*
Can hold, and heare fuch uile detraction ?
Yee Pines of Ida, shake your faire growne height,
For *Ioue* at firft dash will with thunder fight.

                       Yee

Yee-Cedars bend, fore lightning you difmay,
Ye Lyons tremble, for an Affe doth bray.
Who cannot raile ? what dog but dare to barke
Gainft *Phæbes* brightnes in the filent darke ?
What ftinking Scauenger (if fo he will
Though ftreets be fayre,) but may right eafily fill,
His dungy tumbrel ? fweep, pare, wafh, make cleane,
Yet from your fairnes he fome durt can gleane.
The windie-chollicke ftriu'd to haue fome vent,
And now tis flowne, and now his rage is fpent.
So haue I feene the fuming waues to fret,
And in the end, naught but white foame beget.
So haue I feene the fullen clowdes to cry,
And weepe for anger that the earth was dry
After theyr fpight, that all the haile-fhot drops
Could neuer peirce the chriftiall water tops,
And neuer yet could worke her more difgrace
But onely bubble quiet *Thetis* face.
Vaine enuious detractor from the good
What *Cynicke* fpirit rageth in thy blood ?
Cannot a poore miftaken title fcape
But thou muft that into thy Tumbrell fcrape ?
Cannot fome lewd, immodeft beaftlines
Lurke, and lie hid in iuft forgetfulnes,
But *Grillus* fubtile-fmelling fwinifh fnout
Muft fent, and grunt, and needes will finde it out ?
Come daunce yee ftumbling Satyres by his fide
If he lift once the Syon Mufe deride.
Ye *Granta's* white Nymphs come, and with you bring
Some fillabub, whilft he doth fweetly fing
Gainft *Peters* teares, and *Maries* mouing meane,
And like a fierce enraged Boare doth foame

A₃

At facred Sonnets.   O daring hardiment!
At *Bartas* fweet *Semaines*, raile impudent
At *Hopkins*, *Sternhold*, and the *Scottish* King,
At all Tranflators that do ftriue to bring
That ftranger language to our vulgar tongue,
Spett in thy poyfon theyr fair afts among.
Ding them all downe from faire Ierufalém,
And mew them vp in thy deferued Bedlem.

Shall Painims honor, their vile falfod gods
With fprightly wits? and fhall not we by ods
Farre, farre, more ftriue with wits beft quinteffence
To adore that facred euer-liuing Effence?
Hath not ftrong reafon moou'd the Legifta mind,
To fay the fayreft of all Natures kinde
The Prince by his prerogatiue may claime?
Why may not then our foules without thy blame
(Which is the beft thing that our God did frame)
Deuote the beft part to his facred Name?
And with due reuérence and deuotion
Honor his Name with our inuention?
No, Poefie not fit for fuch an action,
It is defil'd with fuperftition:
It honord Baal, therefore poluta, polute,
Unfit for fuch a facred inftitute.
So haue I heard an Hæretick maintaine
The Church vnholy, where *Iehouas* Name
Is now ador'd: Becaufe he furely knowes
Some-times it was defil'd with Popifh fhowes.
The Bells profane, and not to be endur'd,
Becaufe to Popifh rites they were inur'd.
Pure madnes peace, ceafe to be infolent;
And be not outward fober, inlye impudent.

Fie

Fie inconfiderate, it greeueth me
An Academick fhould fo fenceles be.
Fond Cenfurer! Why fhould thofe mirrors feeme
So vile to thee? Which better iudgements deeme
Exquifite then, and in our polifh'd times
May run for fenefull tollerable lines.
What, not *mediocria firma* from thy fpight?
But muft thy enuious hungry fangs needs light
On *Magiftrates mirrour?* Muft thou needs detract
And ftriue to worke his antient honors wrack?
What, fhall not *Refamund, or Galefon,*
Ope their fweet lips without detraction?
But muft our moderne *Crittick* enuious eye
Seeme thus to quote fome groffe deformity?
Where Art, not error fhineth in their ftile,
But error, and no Art doth thee beguile.
For tell me *Crittick, is not Fiction*
The foule of Poefie inuention?
Is't not the forme, the fpirit, and the effence?
The life, and the effentiall difference?
Which *omni, femper, foli,* doth agree
To heauenly difcended Poefie?
Thy wit God comfort mad *Chirurgion*
What, make fo dangerous an Incifion?
At firft dafh whip away the inftrument
Of Poets Procreation? fie ignorant!
When as the foule, and vitall-blood doth reft
And hath in *Fiction* onely intereft?
What *Satyre!* fucke the foule from Poefie
And leaue him fpritles? O impiety!
Would euer any *erudite Pedant*
Seeme in his artles lines fo infolent?

O   But

But thus it is when pitty Priscians
Will needs step vp to be Censorians.
When once they can in true skan'd verses frame
A braue Encomium *of good Vertues name.*
Why thus it is, when Mimick Apes will striue
With Iron wedge the trunks of Oakes to riue.
　　But see, his spirit of detraction
Must nible at a glorious action.
Euge! some gallant spirit, some resolued blood
Will hazard all to worke his Countries good
And to enrich his soule, and raise his name
Will boldly saile vnto the rich *Gaiane.*
What then ? must straight some shameles Satyrist
With odious and opprobious termes insist
To blast so high resolu'd intention
With a malignant vile detraction?
So haue I seene a curre dogge in the streete
Pisse gainst the fairest posts he still could meete.
So haue I seen the march wind striue to fade
The fairest hewe that Art, or Nature made.
So Enuy still doth bark at clearest shine
And striues to staine heroick acts, deuine.
Well, I haue cast thy water, and I see
Th'art falne to wits extreamest pouerty,
Sure in Consumption of the spritly part.
Goe vse some Cordiall for to cheere thy hart:
Or els I feare that I one day shall see
Thee fall, into some dangerous Lethargie.
　　But come fond Bragart, crowne thy browes with Bay
Intrance thy selfe in thy sweet extasie.
Come, manumit thy plumie pinion,
And scower the sword of Eluish champion,

Or els vouchfafe to breathe in wax-bound quill,
And daine our longing eares with mufick fill:
Or let vs fee thee fome fuch ftanzaes frame
That thou maift raife thy vile inglorious name.
Summon the Nymphs and Driades to bring
Some rare inuention, whilft thou dooft fing
So fweet, that thou *maift fhoulder from aboue*
The Eagle from the ftaires of friendly Ioue :
And leade fad Pluto Captiue *with thy fong,*
Gracing thy felfe, that art obfcur'd fo long.
Come fomewhat fay (but hang me when tis done)
Worthy of braffe, and hoary marble ftone ;
Speake yee attentiue Swaines that heard him neuer
Will not his Paftorals indure for euer?
Speake yee that neuer heard him ought but raile
Doe not his Poems beare a glorious faile?
Hath not he ftrongly iuftled from aboue
The Eagle from the ftaires of friendly Ioue?
May be, may be, tut tis his modefty,
He could if that he would, nay would if could I fee.
Who cannot raile?, and with a blafting breath
Scorch euen the whiteft Lillies of the earth?
Who cannot ftumble in a ftuttering ftile?
And fhallow heads with *feeming fhades* beguile?
Ceafe, ceafe, at length to be maleuolent,
To faireft bloomes of Vertues eminent.
Striue not to foile the frefheft hewes on earth
With thy malitious and vpbraiding breath.
Enuie, let Pines of *Ida* reft alone,
For they will growe fpight of thy thunder ftone,
Striue not to nible in their fwelling graine
With toothles gums of thy detracting braine :

O 2   Rate

Eate not thy dam, but laugh and fport with me
At ftrangers follies with a merry glee,
Lets not maligne our kin. Then Satyrift.
I doe falute thee with an open fift.

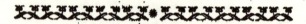

SATYRE V.

Parua magna, magna nulla.

AMbitious *Gorgons,* wide-mouth'd *Lamians,*
Shape-changing *Proteans,* damn'd *Briarians,*
Is *Minos* dead, is *Radamanth* a floepe;
That yee thus dare vnto *Ioues* Pallace creepe?
What, hath *Ramnusia* fpent her knotted whip?
That yee dare ftriue on *Hebes* cup to fip?
Yet know *Apolloes* quiuer is not fpent
But can abate your daring hardiment.
Python is flaine, yet his accurfed race,
Dare looke diuine *Aftrea* in the face:
Chaos returne, and with confufion
Inuolue the world with ftrange difunion:
For *Pluto* fits in that adored chaire
Which doth belong vnto *Minruas* heire.
O Hecatombe! O Cataftrophe!   *Hæc vf-*
From *Mydas* pompe, to *Irus* beggery!   *que Xili-*
Prometheus, who celeftiall fier   *num.*
Did fteale from heauen, therewith to infpire
Our earthly bodies with a fence-full minde,
Whereby we might the depth of Nature find.

                                        Is

Is ding'd to hell, and vulture eates his hart
Which did such deepe Philosophy impart
To mortall men. When theeuing *Mercury*
That euen in his new borne infancy
Stole faire *Apollos* quiuer, and *Ioues* mace,
And would haue filch'd the lightning from his place,
But that he fear'd he should haue burnt his wing
And sing'd his downy feathers new come spring;
He that in gastly shade of night doth leade
Our soules, vnto the empire of the dead.
When he that better doth deserue a rope
Is a faire planet in our Horoscope.
And now hath *Caduceus* in his hand
Of life and death that hath the sole command.
Thus petty thefts are payed, and soundly whipt,
But greater crimes are slightly ouerslipt:
Nay he's a God that can doe villany
With a good grace, and glib facility.

  The harmles hunter, with a ventrous eye
When vnawares he did *Diana* spie,
Nak'd in the fountaine he became straightway
Vnto his greedy hounds a wished pray,
His owne delights taking away his breath,
And all ungratefull forc'd his fatal death.
(And euer since Hounds eate their Maisters cleane,
For so *Diana* curst them in the streame.)
When strong backt *Hercules* in one poore night
With great, great ease, and wondrous delight
In strength of lust and *Uenus* surquedry
Rob'd fifty wenches of virginity.
Farre more than lusty *Laurence*, Yet poore soule
He with *Acteon* drinks of *Nemis* bole,

O 3   When

When *Hercules* lewd act, is regiſtred,
And for his fruitfull labour Deified.
And had a place in heaven him aſſigned .
When he the world, vnto the world reſigned.
Thus little ſcapes are deepely puniſhed,
But mighty villanes are for Gods adored.
Ioue brought his ſiſter to a nuptiall bed,
And hath an *Hebe*, and a *Ganemede*,
A *Leda* and a thouſand more beſide,
His chaſte *Alomena*, and his ſiſter bride :
Who fore his face was odiouſly defil'd
And by *Ixion* groſely got with child.
This thunderer, that right vertuouſly
Thruſt forth his father from his empery
Is now the great Monarko of the earth,
Whoſe awfull nod, whoſe all commaunding breath
Shakes Europe's ground-worke §.   And his title makes
As dread a noyſe, as when a Canon ſhakes
The ſubtile ayre.   Thus hell-bred villany
Is ſtill rewarded with high dignity.
When *Siſyphus* that did but once reueale
That this inceſtious villaine had to deale
In Ile *Phliunta* with *Egina* faire,
Is damn'd to hell, in endles black diſpaire
Euer to reare his tumbling ſtone vpright
Vpon the ſteepy mountaines lofty height.
His ſtone will neuer now get greeniſh moſſe
Since he hath thus encur'd ſo great a loſſe
As *Ioues* high fauour.   But it needs muſt be
Whilſt *Ioue* doth rule, and ſway the empery

§ *Rex hominumque Deorumque.*

And

And poore *Aftrea's* fled into an Ile
And liues a poore and banifhed exile:
And there pen'd vp, fighs in her fad lament,
Wearing away in pining languifhment.
If that *Sylenus* Affe doe chaunce to bray,
And fo the Satyres lewdnes doth bewray,
Let him for euer be a facrifice;
Pricke, fpurre, beate, loade, for euer tyranife
Ouer the foole, But let fome *Carberus*
Keepe back the wife of fweet tongu'd *Orpheus*,
Gnato applaudes the Hound. Let that fame child
Of Night and Sleepe, (which hath the world defil'd,
With odious railing) barke gainft all the work
Of all the Gods, and find fome error lurke
In all the graces. Let his lauer lip
Speake in reproach of Natures workmanfhip,
Let him vpbraid faire *Venus* if he lift
For her fhort heele. Let him with rage infift
To fnarle at *Vulcans* minz, becaufe he was
Not made with windowes of tranfparant glas,
That all might fee the paffions of his mind.
Let his all-blafting tongue great errors find
In *Pallas* houfe, becaufe if next fhould burne
It could not from the fodaine perill turne.
Let him vpbraide great *Ioue* with luxury
Condemne the Heauens Queene of ieloufie.
Yet this fame Stygian *Memus* muft be prayfed
And to fome Godhead at the leaft be raifed.
But if poor *Orpheus* fing melodioufly,
And ftriue with muficks fweeteft fymphonie
To praife the Gods, and vnaduifedly
Doe but ore-flip one drunken Deitie,

Forthwith

Forthwith the bouzing *Bacchus* out doth send
His furious *Bacchides*, to be reueng'd.
And straight they teare the sweet Musitian,
And leaue him to the dogs diuision.
Hebrus, beare witnes of their crueltie,
For thou did'st view poore *Orpheus* tragedi.
Thus slight neglects are deepest villanie,
But blasting mouthes deserue a deitie.
Since *Gallus* slept, when he was set to watch
Least *Sol* or *Uulcan* should *Mauortius* catch
In using *Venus*: since the boy did nap,
Whereby bright *Phœbus* did great *Mars* intrap.
Poore *Gallus* now, (whilom to *Mars* so deere)
Is turned to a crowing Chaunteclere;
And euer since, fore that the sun doth shine,
(Least *Phœbus* should with his all-peircing eyne
Discry some *Uulcan*,) he doth crow full shrill,
That all the ayre with Ecchoes he doth fill.
Whilst *Mars*, though all the Gods do see his sin,
And know in what lewd vice he liueth in,
Yet is adored still, and magnified,
And with all honors duly worshipped.
Euge! small faults to mountaines straight are raised,
Slight scapes are whipt, but damned deeds are praised.
  Fie, fie, I am deceiued all thys while,
A mist of errors doth my sence beguile;
I haue beene long of all my witts bereauen,
Heauen for hell taking, taking hell for heauen;
Vertue for vice, and vice for vertue still,
Sower for sweet, and good for passing ill.
If not? Would vice and odious villanie
Be still rewarded with high dignity?

                                        Would

Would damned *Ionians*, be of all men praifed,
And with high honors vnto heauen raifed?
  Tis fo, tis fo; Riot, and Luxurie
Are vertuous, meritorious chaftitie:
That which I thougt to be damn'd hel-borne pride
Is humble modeftie, and nought befide;
That which Idee med *Bacchus* furquedry,
Is graue, and ftaied, civill, *Sobrietie*.
O then thrice holy age, thrice facred men!
Mong whom no vice a Satyre can difcerne,
Since Luft is turned into *Chaftitie*,
And Riot, vnto fad *Sobrietie*.
Nothing but goodnes raigneth in our age,
And vertues all are ioyn'd in marriage.
Heere is no dwelling for Impiety,
No habitation for bafe Villanie.
Heere are no fubiects for *Reproofes* fharpe vaine,
Then hence rude Satyre, make away amaine;
And feeke a feate where more Impuritie
Doth lye and lurke in ftill fecuritie.
  Now doth my Satyre ftagger in a doubt,
Whether to ceafe, or els to write it out.
The fubiect is too fharpe for my dull quill.
Some fonne of *Maya* fhow thy riper fkill.
For Ile goe turne my tub againft the funne,
And wiftly marke how higher Plannets runne,
Contemplating their hidden motion.
Then on fome *Latmos* with *Endimion*,
I'le flumber out my time in difcontent,
And neuer wake to be maleuolent,
A beedle to the worlds impuritie;
But euer fleepe in ftill fecuritie.

                                    If thys

If thys difpleafe the worlds wrong-iudging fight,
. It glads my foule, and in fome better fpright
I'le write againe.   But if that this doe pleafe,
Hence, hence, Satyrick Mufe, take endleffe eafe.
Hufh now yee Band-doggs, barke no more at me,
But let me flide away in fecrecie.

                              EPICTETUS.

AT LONDON,
Printed by *Iames Roberts.*   1598.

THE

SCOVRGE

OF

VILLANIE.

Three Bookes of SATYRES.

By JOHN MARSTON.

Nec fcombros metuentia carmina, nec thus.

PERSIUS.

AT LONDON,
Printed by I. R. Anno Dom.
1599.
Reprinted 1764.

To his most esteemed, and best beloved
Selfe.

DAT DEDICATQUE.

TO

DETRACTION I prefent my POESIE.

FOule canker of faire vertuous action,
  Vile blafter of the frefheft bloomes on earth,
Enuies abhorred childe, *Detraction*,
I here expofe, to thy al-tainting breath,
  The iffue of my braine: fnarle, raile, barke, bite,
  Knowe that my fpirit fcornes *Detractions* fpight.

Knowe that the *Genius*, which attendeth on,
And guides my powers intellectuall,
Holds in all vile repute *D.traction*,
My foule an effence metaphyficall,
  That in the bafeft fort fcornes *Critickes* rage,
  Becaufe he knowes his facred parentage.

My fpirit is not puft vp with fatte fume
Of flimie Ale, nor *Bacchus* heating grape.
My minde difdaines the dungy muddy fcum
Of abiect thoughts, and *Enuies* raging hate.
  True iudgement flight regards Opinion,
  A fprightly wit difdaines Detraction.

A partiall praife fhall neuer eleuate
My fetled cenfure of my own efteeme.
A cankered verdit of malignant hate
Shall nere prouoke me, worfe my felfe to deeme.
  Spight of defpight, and rancors villanie,
  I am my felfe, fo is my poefie.

❦❦❦❦❦❦❦❦❦❦❦❦❦❦❦❦❦❦❦❦❦❦❦❦❦❦

In Lectores prorsus indignos.

FY Satyre fie, shall each mechanick slaue,
Each dunghill pesant, free perusall haue.
Of thy well labor'd lines? Each sattin sute,
Each quaint fashion-monger, whose sole repute
Rests in his trim gay clothes, lie slaucring
Tainting thy lines with his lewd censuring?
Shall each odde puisne of the Lawyers Inne,
Each banny-froth, that last day did beginne
To read his little, or his *nere a whit*,
Or shall some greater auntient, of lesse wit
(That neuer 'turn'd but browne Tobacco leaues,
Whose sences some damn'd *Occupant* bereaues)
Lye gnawing on thy vacant times expence?
Tearing thy rimes, quite altering the sence?
Or shall perfum'd *Castilio* censure thee?
Shall he oreview thy sharpe-fang'd poesie?
(Who nere read further than his Mistresse lips)
Nere practiz'd ought, but som spruce capring skips
Nere in his life did other language vse,
But *sweet Lady, faire Mistris, kind Hart, deere Cuz,*
Shall this *Fantasma,* this *Colosse* peruse,
And blast with stinking breath, my budding Muse?
Fie, wilt thou make thy wit a Curtezan?
For euery broking hand-crafts artizan?
Shall brainlesse Cyterne heads, each iobernole,
Pocket the very *Genius* of thy soule?
I *Phylo,* I, I'le keepe an open hall,
A common, and a sumptuous festiuall.

Welcome

Welcome all eyes, all eares, all tongues to mee,
Gnaw pesants on my scraps of Poesie.
Castilios, *Cyprians*, court-boyes, spanish blocks,
Ribanded eares, Granado-netherstocks,
Fidlers, scriueners, pedlers, tynkering knaues,
Base blew-coates, tapsters, broad-minded slaues
Welcome I-faith: but may you nere depart,
Till I haue made your gauled hides to smart.
Your gauled hides? auaunt base muddy scum.
Thinke you a Satyres dreadful sounding drum
Will brace itselfe? and daine to terrifie
Such abiect pesants basest roguery?
No, no, passe on ye vaine fantasticke troupe
Of puffie youths; Knowe I do scorne to stoupe
To rip your liues. Then hence lewd nags away,
Goe read each poast, view what is plaid to day,
Then to *Priapus* gardens. You *Castilio*,
I pray thee let my lines in freedome goe,
Let me alone, the madams call for thee,
Longing to laugh at thy wits pouerty.
Sirra, liuorie cloake, you lazie slipper slaue,
Thou fawning drudge, what would'st thou Satyres haue?
Base mind away, thy master cals, be gone,
Sweet *Gnato* let my poesie alone.
Goe buy some ballad of the Faiery King,
And of the begger wench, some roguie thing,
Which thou maist chaunt vnto the chamber-maid
To some vile tune, when that thy Master's laid.

But will you needs stay? am I forc't to beare
The blasting breath of each lewd censurer?
Must naught but cloths, and images of men,
But sprightlesse trunks, be Iudges of thy pen?

P 2   Nay

Nay then come all. I proftitute my Mufe,
For all the fwarmes of Idiots to abufe.
Reade all, view all, euen with my full confent,
So you will know that which I neuer meant;
So you will nere conceiue, and yet difpraife,
That which yon nere conceiu'd, and laughter raife
Where I but ftriue in honeft ferioufneffe,
To fcourge fome foule-polluting beaftlineffe.
So you will raile, and finde huge errors lurke
In euery corner of my Cynick worke.
Proface, read on, for your extreamft diflikes
Will adde a pineon, to my praifes flights.
O, how I briftle vp my plumes of pride,
O, how I thinke my Satyres dignifi'd,
When I once heare fome quaint *Gaftilio*,
Some fupple mouth'd flaue, fome lewd *Tubrio*,
Some fpruce pedant, or fome fpan-new come fry
Of Innes a-court, ftriuing to vilefie
My dark reproofes. Then doe but raile at me,
No greater honour craues my poefie.

  1. But ye diuiner wits, celeftiall foules,   (troules,
      Whofe free borne minds no kennell thought con-
Ye facred fpirits, *Mayas* eldeft fonnes,

  2. Yee fubftance of the fhadowes of our age,
     In whom all graces linke in mariage,
To you how cheerefully my Poem runnes.

  3. True iudging eyes, quick fighted cenfurers,
     Heauens beft beauties, wifdomes treafurers,
O how my loue embraceth your great worth!

4. Yee Idols of my soule, yee blessed spirits,
  How shall I giue true honor to your merrits?
Which I can better thinke, then here paint forth.

You sacred spirits, Muias eldest sonnes,
To you how cheerefully my poeme runnes?
O how my loue embraceth your great worth!
Which I can better thinke, then here paint forth.

                                        O rare!

To those that seeme iudiciall Perusers.

Knowe, I hate to affect too much obscuritie and harshi-
nesse, because they profit no sense. To note vices,
so that no man can vnderstand them, is as fond, as the
French execution in picture. Yet there are some (too
many) that thinke nothing good, that is so curteous, as
to come within their reach. Tearming all Satyres bastard) which are not palpable darke, and so rough writ,
that the hearing of them read, would set a mans teeth
on edge. For whose vnseasoned palate I wrote the first
Satyre, in some places too obscure, in all places misly-
ing me. Yet when by some scuruie chaunce it shall
come into the late perfumed fist of iudiciall *Torquatus*,
(that like some rotten sticke in a troubled water, hath
gotte a great deal of barmie froth to stick to his sides) I
knowe hee will vouchsafe it some of his new-minted
Epithets, (as *Reall, Intrinsecate, Delphicks,*) when in my
conscience hee vnderstands not the least part of it. But
from thence proceedes his iudgment. *Persius* is crabby,

                  P 3   because

becaufe auntient, and his ierkes, (being porticularly
given to priuate cuftomes of his time) dufky. *Iuvenall*
(upon the like occafion) feemes to our iudgement, gloomy. Yet both of them goe a good feemely pafe, not
ftumbling, fhuffling. *Chaucer* is hard euen to our vn-
derftandings: who knowes not the reafon? how much
more thofe olde Satyres which expreffe themfelues in
termes, that breathed not long euen in their daies. But
had wee then liued, the vnderftanding of them had beene
nothing hard. I will not deny there is a feemely deco-
rum to be obferued, and a peculiar kinde of fpeech for a
Satyres lips. which I can willinglyer conceiue, then dare
to prefcribe; yet let me haue the fubftance rough, not
the fhadow. I cannot, nay I will not delude your fight
with mifts; yet I dare defend my plaineneffe againft the
veriuice-face, of the Crabbedft Satyrift that euer ftut-
tered. He that thinks worfe of my rimes then my felfe,
I fcorn him, for hee cannot: he that thinks better, is a
foole. So fauour me, *Good opinion*, as I am farre from
being a *Suffenus*. If thou perufeft mee with an vnpar-
tiall eye, reade on: if otherwife, I know I nether value
thee, nor thy cenfure.

W. KINSAYDER.

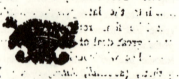

P. R O-

PROEMIUM

IN
LIBRUM PRIMUM.

I Beare the scourge of iust *Rhamnusia*,
Lashing the lewdnesse of *Britannia*.
Let others sing as their good *Genius* moues,
Of deepe designes, or else of clipping loues.
Faire fall them all, that with wits industrie,
Doe cloath good subiectes in true poesie,
But as for me, my vexed thoughtfull soule
Takes pleasure in displeasing sharpe controule.
    Thou nursing Mother of faire wisdomes lore,
Ingenuous Melancholy, I implore
Thy graue assistance: take thy gloomy seate,
Inthrone thee in my blood, let me intreate.
Stay his quicke iocund skips, and force him runne
A sad pas't course, vntill my whips be done.
Daphne, vnclip thine armes from my sad brow,
Blacke Cypresse crowne me, whilst I vp doe plow
The hidden entrailes of rank villany,
Tearing the vaile from damn'd impietie.
    Quake guzzell dogs, that liue on putred slime,
    Skud from the lashes of my yerking rime.

Marry

SATYRE I.

Fronti nulla fides.

Arry God forefend, *Martius* fweares he'le ftab.
Phrigea, feare not, thou art no lying drab.
What though dagger hack'd mouthes of his blade fweares
It flew as many as figures of yeares
Aqua fortis eate in't, or as many more,
As methodift *Mufes* kill with Helfebore
In autumne laft, yet he beares the male fye
With as fmooth calme, as *Mecho* riualrie.
How ill his fhape with inward forme doth fadge,
Like *Aphrogenias* ill-yok't marriage,
Fond Phyfiognomer, *Complexion*
Guides not the inward difpofition,
Inclines I yeeld; Thou fai'ft law *Iulia*,
Or *Catoes* often curft *Scatinia*
Can take no hold on fimpring *Lefbia*,
True, not on her aye: yet Afloni oft doth blaft,
The fprouting bud that faine would longer laft.
Chary *Cafra*, right pure, or *Rbodanus*,
Yet each night drinkes in glaffie Priapus.

Yon pine is faire, yet fouly doth it ill
To his owne fprouts: marke, his rank drops diftill
Foule Naples canker in their tender rinde.
Woe worth when trees drop in their proper kinde.
Miftagogus, what meanes this prodigy?
When *Hiedolgo* fpeakes 'gainft vfury,

When

When *Verres* railes 'gainſt thieues, *Mylo* doth hate
Murder, *Clodius* cuckolds, *Marius* the gate
Of ſquinting *Ianus* ſhuts? Runne beyond bound
Of *Nil vltra,* and hang me when on's found
Will be himſelfe. Had Nature turn'd our eyes
Into our proper ſelues, theſe curious ſpies
Would be aſham'd: *Flavia* would bluſh to flout,
When *Oppia* cals *Lucina* helpe her out.
If ſhe did thinke, *Lynceus* did know her ill,
How Nature Art, how Art doth Nature ſpill.
God pardon me, I often did auer
Quod gratis grate : the Aſtronomer
An honeſt man, but Ile do ſo no more,
His face deceiu'd me; but now, ſince his whore
And ſiſter are all one, his honeſtie
Shall be as bare as his Anatomie,
To which he bound his wife: O packſtaffe rimes !
Why not, when court of ſtars ſhall ſee theſe crimes ?
Rods are in piſſe, I for thee *Empericke,*
That twenty graines of *Oppium* will not ſticke
To miniſter to babes. Heer's bloody daies,
When with plaine hearbes *Mutius* more men ſlaies
Then ere third *Edwards* ſword.   Sooth in our age,
Mad *Coribantes* neede not to enrage
The peoples mindes.   You *Ophiogine*
Of *Helleſpont,* with wrangling villanie
The ſwoln world's inly ſtung, then daine a touch,
If that your fingers can effect ſo much.
Thou ſweete Arabian *Pauchaia,*
Perfume this naſtie age : ſmugge *Leſbia*
Hath ſtinking lunges, although a ſimpring grace,
A muddy inſide, though a ſurphul'd face.

                                         O for

O for some deep-searching *Caryceus*,
To ferret out yon lewd *Cynedian*.

  How now *Brutus*, what shape best pleaseth thee?
All *Protean* formes, thy wife in venery,
At thy inforcement takes? well goe thy way,
Shee may ttansforme thee ere thy dying day.
Hush, *Gracchus* heares; that hath retaild more lyes,
Broched more slaunders, done more villanies,
Then *Fabius* perpetuall golden coate
(Which might haue *Semper idem* for a mott)
Hath been at feasts, and led the measuring
At Court, and in each mariage reueling.
Writ *Palephatus* comment on those dreames,
That *Hylus* takes, midst dung-pit reaking steames
Of *Athos* hote house, Gramercie modest smyle,
Chremes asleepe, *Paphia*, sport the while.
Lucia, new set thy ruffe, tut thou art pure,
Canst thou not lispe, *(good brother)* look demure?
Fye *Gallus*, what, a Skeptick *Pyrrhonist*?
When chast *Dictinna*, breakes the Zonelike twist?
Tut, hang vp *Hieroglyphickes*. Ile not faine
Wresting my humor, from his natiue straine.

✖✖✖✖✖✖✖✖✖✖ ✳ ✖✖✖✖✖✖✖✖✖✖

SATYRE II.

Difficile est Satyram non scribere.
————— *Iuue.*

I Cannot holde, I cannot I indure
  To view a big womb'd foggy clowde immure
The radiant tresses of the quickning sunne,
Let Custards quake, my rage must freely runne.

                        Preach

Preach not the Stoickes patience to me.
I hate no man, but mens impietie.
My foule is vext: what power will refift,
Or dares to ftop a fharpe fang'd Satyrift?
Who'le coole my rage? who'le ftay my itching fift?
But I will plague and torture whom I lift.
If that the three-fold wals of *Babilon*
Should hedge my tongue, yet I fhould raile vpon
This fuftie world, that now dare put in vre
To make *IEHOUA* but a couertute,
To fhade ranck filth. *Loofe confcience is free,*
From all confcience; what els hath libertie?
As't pleafe the Thracian Boreas to blow,
So turnes our ayerie confcience, to, and fro.

  What icye *Saturnift*, what Northerne pate,
But fuch groffe lewdneffe would exafperate?
I thinke, the blind doth fee the flame-God rife
From fifters couch, each morning to the fkies,
Glowing with luft. Walke but in dufkie night,
With *Lynceus* eyes, and to thy piercing fight
Difguifed Gods will fhowe, in pefants fhape,
Preft to commit fome execrable rape.
Here *Ioues* luft-Pandar, *Maias* inggling foone,
In clownes difguife, doth after milk-maids runne,
And, fore he'le loofe his brutifh lechery,
The truls fhall tafte fweet Nectars furquedry.
There *Iunos* brat, forfakes *Neries* bed,
And like a fwaggerer, luft fiered,
  Attended only with his fmock-fworne Page,
Pert *Gallus*, flily flips along, to wage

Titlag

Tilting incounters, with fome fpurious feede
Of marrow pies, and yawning Oyfters breede.
　　　　　　　　　O damn'd!
　Who would not fhake a Satyres knotty rod?
When to defile the facred feate of God
Is but accounted Gentlemens difport?
To fnort in filth, each hower to refort
To brothell pits; alas a veniall crime,
Nay, royall, to be laft in *thirtith* flime.

　Ay me, hard world for Satyrifts beginne
To fet vp fhop, when no fmall petty finne
Is left vnpurg'd.　Once to be purfie fat
Had wont be caufe that life did macerate.
Marry the iealous Queene of ayre doth frowne,
That Ganimede is vp, and Hebe downe.
Once *Albion* liu'd in fuch a cruell age
Than men did hold by feruile villenage,
Poore brats were flaues, of bond-men that were borne,
And marted, fold: but that rude law is torne,
And difannuld, as too too inhumane,
That Lords ore pefants fhould fuch feruice ftraine.
*But now, (fad change!) the kennell fucke of flaues
Pefant great Lords, and feruile feruice craues.*

　Bondflaue fonnes had wont be bought and fold:
But now *Heroes* heires (if they haue not told
A difcreet number, 'fore their dad did die)
Are made much of: how much from merchandie?
Tail'd, and retail'd, till to the pedlers packe,
The fourth-hand ward-ware comes: alack, alack.
*Would truth did know I lyed: but truth, and I
Doe know that fenfe is borne to mifery.*

　　　　　　　　　Oh would

Oh would to God, this were their worst mischance,
Were not their soules sould to darke ignorance.
Fair godnes is foul ill, if mischiefes wit
Be not represt from lewd corrupting it.

   O what dry braine melts not sharp mustard rime,
To purge the snottery of our slimie time!
Hence idle *Caue.*   Vengeance pricks me on,
When mart is made of faire Religion.
Reform'd bald *Trebus* swore, in Romish quiet,
He sold Gods essence for a poor denier.
The Egyptians adored Onions,
To Garlike yeelding all deuotions.
O happie Garlike, but thrice happie you,
Whose senting gods in your large gardens grew.
Democritus, rise from thy putred slime,
Sport at the madnesse of that hotter clime,
Deride their frenzy, that for policie
Adore Wheate dough, as reall deitie.
Almighty men, that can their maker make,
And force his sacred bodie to forsake
The Cherubins, to be gnawns actually,
Diuiding *indiuiduum,* really:
Making a score of Gods, with one poore word.
I, so I thought, in that you could afford,
So cheape a penny-worth.   O ample field,
In which a Satyre may iust weapon weelde.
But I am vext, when swarmes of *Iulians*
Are stil manur'd by lewd Precisians.
Who scorning Church rites, take the symbole vp,
As slouenly, as carelesse Courtiers slup
Their mutton gruell.   Fie, who can with-hold,
But must of force make his mild muse a scold?

       Q   When

When that hee greeued fees, with red vext eyes,
That Athens antient large immunities
Are eyefores to the Fates.   Poore eels forlorne,
Ift not enough you are made an abieét fcorne
To ieering apes, but muft the fhadow too
Of auncient fubftance, be thus wrung from you!
O fplit my heart, leaft it doe breake with rage,
To fee th'immodeft loofeneffe of our age.
Immodeft loofeneffe? fie, too gentle word,
When euery figne can brothelry afford:
When luft doth fparkle from our females eyes,
And modeftie is roufted in the fkyes.
    Tell me *Galliottæ*, what meanes this figne,
When impropriat gentles will turne *Capuchine?*
Sooner be damn'd.   O ftuffe Satyricall!
When rapine feeds our pomp, pomp ripes our fall:
When the gueft trembles at his hofts fwart looke,
The fon doth feare his ftepdame, that hath tooke
His mothers place, for luft: the twin-borne brother
Malignes his mate, that firft came from his mother.
When to be huge, is to be deadly ficke.
When vertuous pefants will not fpare to lick
The diuels taile for poore promotion.
When for negleét, flubbred *Deuotion*
Is wan with griefe.   When *Rufus* yauns for death
Of him that gaue him vndeferued breath.
When *Hermus* makes a worthy queftion,
Whether of *Wright*, as *Paraphonalion*
A filuer piffe-pot fits his Lady dame?
Or is't too good? a pewter beft became.
When *Agrippina* poyfons *Claudius* fonne,
That all the world to her owne brat might run.

                                    When

When the hufband gapes that his ftale wife would dy,
That he might once be in by *Curtifie.*
The big paunch't wife longs for her loth'd mates death,
That fhe might haue more ioyntures here on earth.
When tenure for fhort yeares (by many a one)
Is thought right good be turn'd forth *Littleton,*
All to be *beaddy,* or *free-bold* at leaft,
When tis all one, for long life be a beaft,
A flaue, as haue a fhort term'd tenancie.
When dead's the ftrength of Englands yeomanry;
When invndation of luxurioufneffe
Fats all the world with fuch groffe beaftlineffe,
Who can abftaine? what modeft braine can hold,
But he muft make his fhamefac'd Mufe a fcold?

S A T Y R E   III.

Redde, age, quæ deinceps rififti.

IT's good be warie, whilft the funne fhines cleer;
(Quoth that old chuffe, that may difpend by yeer
Three thoufand pound) whil'ft hee of good pretence
Commits himfelfe to Fleet, to faue expence.
No Countries Chriftmas: rather tarry heere,
The Fleete is cheap, the country hall too deere.
But *Codrus,* harke, the world expects to fee
Thy baftard heire rot there in mifery.
What? will *Luxurio* keepe fo great a hall,
That he will prooue a baftard in his fall?

Q 2   No:

No: *come on fiue* : *S. George, by heauen at all*
Makes his cataſtrophe right tragicall.
At all? till nothings left: *Come on,* till all comes off,
I haire and all: *Luxurie* left a ſcoffe
To leaprous filths: O ſtay, thou impious ſlaue,
Teare not the lead from off thy fathers graue,
To ſtop baſe brokeage: fell not thy fathers ſheet,
His leaden ſheet; that ſtrangers eyes may greete
Both putrifaction of thy greedy Sire;
And thy abhorred viperous deſire.
But wilt thou needs, ſhall thy Dads lacky brat
Weare thy Sires halfe-rot finger in his hat?
Nay then *Luxurie* waſte in obloquie,
And I ſhall ſport to heare thee faintly cry;
A die, a drab, and filthy broking knaues
Are the worlds wide mouthes, all deuouring graues.
Yet *Samus* keepes a right good houſe I heare.
No, it keepes him, and free'th him from chill feare
Of ſhaking fits.　How then ſhall his ſmug wench,
How ſhall her bawd (fit time) aſſiſt her quench
Her ſanguine heate? *Lynceus,* canſt thou ſent?
She hath her Monkey, and her inſtrument
Smooth fram'd at *Uitrio.* O greeuous miſery!
Luſtus hath left her female luxury.
I, it left him; No, his old Cynick Dad
Hath forc't him cleane forſake his Pickhatch drab.
Alack, alack, what peece of luſtfull fleſh.
Hath *Luſcus* left, his *Priape* to redreſſe?
Grieue not good ſoule, he hath his *Ganimede,*
His perfum'd ſhe-goat, ſmooth kembd and high fod.
At Hogſon now his monſtrous luſt he feaſts,
For there he keepes a baudy-houſe of beaſts.

Paphus

Paphus, let *Luscus* haue his Curtezan,
Or we fhall haue a monfter of a man.
Tut, *Paphus* now detaines him from that bower,
And clafps him clofe within his brick-built tower.
Diogenes, thou art damn'd for thy lewd wit,
For *Luscus* now hath fkill to practife it.
Faith what cares he for faire *Cynedian* boyes?
Veluet cap't Goats, dutch Mares? tut common toies,
Detaine them all, on this condition.
He may but ufe the Cynick friction.
  O now ye male ftewes, I can giue pretence
For your luxurious incontinence.
Hence, hence, ye falfed, feeming Patriotes,
Returne not with pretence of faluing fpots,
When here yee foyle vs with impuritie,
And monftrous filth of Doway feminary.
What though *Iberia* yeeld you libertie,
To fnort in fource of Sodome villany?
What though the bloomes of young nobilitie,
Committed to your *Rodons* cuftodie,
Yee *Nero* like abufe? yet nere approche,
Your new *S. Homers* lewdnes here to broche;
Taynting our Townes, and hopefull Academes,
With your luft-bating moft abhorred meanes.
  Valladolid, our Athens gins to tafte
Of thy rank filth. Camphire and Lettuce chafte
Are clean cafheird, now *Sophi* Ringoes eate,
Candi'd Potatoes are Athenians meate.
Hence Holy-thiftle, come fweete marrow pie,
Inflame our backs to itching luxurie.
A Crabs bak't guts, a Lobfters butterd thigh,
I heare them fweare is bloud for venerie.

Had I some snout-faire brats, they should indure
The new found *Castilion* callenture,
Before some pedant Tutor, in his bed,
Should vse my frie, like Phrigian *Ganimede*.
Nay then chaste cels, when greasie *Aretine*,
For his rank *Fico*, is sirnam'd diuine.
Nay then come all yee veniall scapes to me,
I dare well warrant, you'le absolued be.
Rufus, I'le terme thee but intemperate,
I will not once thy vice exaggerate:
Though that each howra thou lowdly swaggerest,
And at the quarter day, pay'st interest
For the forbearance of thy chalked score:
Though that thou keep'st a taly with thy whore:
Since *Nero* keepes his mother *Agrippine*,
And no strange lust can satiate *Messalina*.
  Tullus goe scotfree, though thou often bragst,
That for a *false French-Crowne*, thou vaulting haddst;
Though that thou know'st, for thy incontinence,
Thy drab repaid thee true French pestilence.
But tush, his boast I beare, when *Tigran*
Brags that hee foystes his rotten Curtezan
Vpon his heire, that must haue all his lands:
And them hath ioyn'd in *Hymens* sacred bands.
I'le winke at *Robrus*, that for vicinage
Enters common, on his next neighbors stage:
When *Ioue* maintaines his sister and his whore;
And she incestuous, iealous euermore,
Least that *Europa* on the Bull should ride:
Woe worth, when beasts for filth are deifid.
  Alacke poore rogues, what Censor interdicts
The veniall scapes of him that purses picks?

                                   When

When some flie, golden-flopt *Caftilio*
Can cut a manors ftrings at Primero?
Or with a pawne, fhall giue a Lordfhip mate;
In ftatute ftaple chaining faft his ftate?
   What Academick ftarued Satyrift
Would gnaw rear'd Bacon? or, with lake-black fift,
Would toffe each mock-heap, for fome out-caft fcraps
Of halfe-dung bones, to ftop his yawning chaps?
Or, with a hungry hollow halfe-pin'd iaw,
Would once, a thrice-turn'd, bone-pickt fubiect gnaw?
When fwarmes of Mountebanks, and Bandeti
Damn'd Briareans, finks of villanie,
Factors for lewdnes, Brokers for the deuill,
Infect our foules with all polluting euill.
   Shall *Lucia* fcorne her hufbands luke-warm bed?
(Becaufe her pleafure, being hurried
In ioulting Coach, with glaffe inftrument,
Doth farre exceede the *Phyfitian* blandifhment).
Whilft I (like to fome mute *Pythagorian*)
Halter my hate, and ceafe to curfe and ban
Such brutifh filthe? Shall *Mavio* raife his fame,
By printing pamphlets in anothers name,
And in them praife himfelfe, his wit, his might,
All to be deem'd his Countries Lanthorne light?
Whilft my tongues tyde with bonds of blufhing fhame,
For fear of broching my concealed name?
Shall *Balbus*, the demure Athenian,
Dreame of the death of next *Vicarian?*
Caft his natiuitie? marke his complexion?
Waigh well his bodies weake condition?
That, with guile fleight, he may be fure to get
The Planets place, when his dim fhine fhall fet?

Shall

Shall *Curio* ftreake his lims on his daies couch,
In Sommer bower? and with bare groping touch
Incenfe his luft, confuming all the yeere
In *Cyprian* dalliance, and in *Belgick* cheere?
Shall *Faunus* fpend a hundred gallions
Of Goates pure milke, to laue his ftalions,
As much Rofe iuyce? O bath! O royall, rich
To fcower *Faunus*, and his faut proud bitch.
And when all's cleans'd, fhal the flaues infide ftinke
Worfe than the new caft flime of *Thames* ebd brink;
Whilft I fecurely let him ouer-flip,
Nere yerking him with my Satyricke whip?

Shall *Crifpus* with hypocrifie beguile,
Holding a candle to fome fiend a while?
Now Iew, then Turke, then feeming Chriftian,
Then Athifte, Papift, and ftraight Puritan,
Now nothing, any thing, euen what you lift,
So that fome guilt may greafe his greedy fift?

Shall *Damas* vfe his third-hand ward as iff
As any iade that tuggeth in the mill?
What, fhall law, nature, vertue be reiected?
Shall thefe world Arteries be foule-infected,
With corrupt bloud? Whilft I fhal *Martia* tafke?
Or fome young *Villius*, all in choller afke,
How he can keepe a lazie waiting man,
And buy a hoode, and filuer-handled fan,
With fortie pound? Or fnarle at *Lollios* fonne;
That with induftrious paines hath harder wonne
His true got worfhip, and his gentries name,
Then any Swine-heards brat, that loufie came
To lufkifh Athens: and, with farming pots,
Compiling beds, and fcouring greafie fpots,

By

By chance (when he can like taught Parrat cry,
Deerely belou'd, with simpering grauitie)
Hath got the farme of some gelt Vicary,
And now on cock-horse, gallops iollily;
Tickling with some stolne stuffe his senselesse cure,
Belching lewd termes gainst all sound littrature.
Shall I with shadowes fight? talke bitterly
Romes filth? scraping base channell roguerie?
Whilst such huge Gyants shall affright our eyes
With execrable, damn'd impieties?
Shall I finde trading *Mecbo,* neuer loath.
Frankly to take a damning periured oath?
Shall *Furia* brooke her sisters modesty,
And prostitute her soule to brothelry?
Shall *Cossus* make his well-fac't wife a stale,
To yeeld his braided ware a quicker sale?
Shall cock-horse, fat-pauncht *Milo* staine whole stocks
Of well borne soules, with his adultering spots?
Shall broking Pandars sucke Nobilitie?
Soyling faire stems with foul impuritie?
Nay, shall a trencher slaue extenuate
Some *Lucrece* rape? and straight magnificate
Lewde *Iouian* lust? Whilst my Satyrick vaine
Shall muzled be, not daring out to straine
His tearing paw? No, gloomy *Iuuenall,*
Though to thy fortunes I disastrous fall.

SATYRE IV.

CRAS.

I Marry Sir, here's perfect honeſty,
  When *Martius* will forſweare all villany,
(All damn'd abuſe of paiment in the warres,
All filching from his prince and Souldiers)
When once he can but ſo much bright dirt gleane,
As may maintaine one more White-friers queane,
One drab more, faith then farewell villany,
He'le cleanſe himſelfe to Shoreditch puritie.
  As for *Stadius,* I thinke he hath a ſoule:
And if he were but free from ſharpe controule
Of his ſower hoſt, and from his Taylors bill,
He would not thus abuſe his riming ſkill;
Iading our tired eares with fooleries,
Greaſing great ſlaues, with oyly flatteries:
Good faith I thinke, he would not ſtriue to fute
The back of humorous Time (for baſe repute,
Mong dunghill peſants) botching vp ſuch ware,
As may be ſalable in Sturbridge fare.
If he were once but freed from ſpecialty:
But ſooth, till then, beare with his balladry.
  I aſk't lewd *Gallus* when he'le ceaſe to ſweare,
And with whole-culuerin, raging oaths to teare
The vault of heauen; ſpitting in the eyes
Of natures Nature, lothſome blaſphemies.

T

To morrow, he doth vow he will forbeare.
Next day I meete him, but I heare him sweare
Worfe then before: I put his vowe in minde.
He anfwerrs me, *to morrow;* but I finde,
He fweares next day, farre worfe then ere before;
Putting me off, with *morrow* euermore.
Thus when I vrge him, with his fophiftrie
. He thinkes to falue his damned periury.

    Sylenus now is old, I wonder, I
He doth not hate his triple venerie.
Cold, writhled Eld, his liues-wet almoft fpent,
Me thinkes a vnitie were competent:
But O faire hopes! he whifpers fecretly,
When it leaues him, he'le leaue his lechery.

    When fimpring *Flaccus* (that demurely goes
Right neatly tripping on his new blackt toes)
Hath made rich vfe of his Religion,
Of God himfelfe, in pure deuotion:
When that the ftrange *Ideas* in his head
(Broched 'mongft curious fots, by fhadowes led)
Haue furnifh't him, by his hore auditors
Of faire demeafnes, and goodly rich mannors,
Sooth then he will repent, when's treafury
Shall force him to difclaime his herefie.
What will not poore neede force? But being fped,
God for vs all, the gurmonds paunch is fed:
His mind is chang'd: but when will he doe good?
To morrow: *I, to morrow, by the Rood.*

    Yet *Rufcus* fweares, he'le ceafe to broke a fute:
By peafant meanes ftriuing to get repute,
Mong puffie Spunges, when the Fleet's defraid,
His reuell tier, and his Laundreffe paid.

                                     There

There is a crewe which I too plaine could name,
If so I might without th' *Aquinians* blame,
That lick the tail of greatnesse with their lips :
Laboring with third-hand iests, and Apish skips,
Retayling others wit, long barrelled,
To glib some great mans eares, till panch be fed :
Glad if themselues, as sporting fooles, be made,
To get the shelter of some high-growne shade.
To morrow, yet these base tricks they'le cast off,
And cease for lucre be a ieering spoffe.
Ruscus will leaue, when once he can renue
His wasted clothes, that are asham'd to view
The worlds proud eyes, *Drusus* wil cease to fawne,
When that his Farme, that leaks in melting pawne,
Some Lord-applauded iest hath once set free.
All will *to morrow* leaue there roguery.
When fox-furd *Mecho* (by damn'd vsury,
Cutthrote deceite, and his crafts villany)
Hath rak't together some foul thousand pound,
To make his smug gurle beare a humming sound
In a young merchants eare, faith then (may be)
He'le ponder if there be a Deitie;
Thinking, if to the Parish pouerty,
At his wisht death, be dol'd a half-penny,
A worke of Supererogation,
A good filth-cleansing strong purgation.
  Aulus will leaue begging Monopolies,
When that 'mong troopes of gaudy Butter-flies,
He is but able iet it iollily,
In pie-bald sutes of proud Court brauery.
  To morrow doth *Luxurio* promise me,
He will vnline himselfe from bitchery.

                       Marry

Marry *Alcides* thirteenth act muſt lend
A glorious period, and his luſt-itch end.
When once he hath froth-foaming *Ætna* paſt,
At one an thirtie being alwaies laſt.

If not to *Day* (quoth that *Naſonian*)
Much leſſe *to morrow*. Yes ſaith *Fabian:*
For ingrain'd Habits, *died with often dips,*
Are not ſo ſoone diſcoloured. Young ſlips
New ſet, are eaſily mou'd, and pluck't away:
But elder rootes clip faſter in the clay.
I ſmile at thee, and at the Stagerite:
Who holds, the liking of the appetite,
Being fed with actions often put in vre,
Hatcheth the ſoule, in quality impure,
Or pure. May be in vertue: but for vice,
That comes by inſpiration, with a trice.
Young *Furius* ſcarce fifteen yeares of age
But is, ſtraight-waies, right fit for marriage,
Vnto the diuell: for ſure they would agree;
Betwixt their ſoules their is ſuch ſympathy.

O where's your ſweatie habit? when each Ape,
That can but ſpy the ſhadowe of his ſhape,
That can no ſooner ken what's vertuous,
But will auoid it, and be vitious.
Without much doe, or farre fetch't habiture,
In earneſt thus; *It is a ſacred cure*
To ſalue the ſoules dread wounds, Omnipotent
That Nature is, that cures the impotent,
Euen in a moment, Sure, Grace is infus'd
By diuine fauour, not by actions us'd.
Which is as permanent as heauens bliſſe
To them that haue it, then no habit is,

R

To morrow, nay, to day, it may be got.
So pleafe that gratious Power cleanfe thy fpot.
   Vice, from priuation of that facred Grace,
Which God with-drawes, but puts not vice in place.
Who faies the funne is caufe of vgly night?
Yet when he vailes our eyes from his faire fight,
The gloomy curtaine of the night is fpred,
Yee curious fotts, vainely by Nature led,
Where is your vice, or vertuous habite now?
For, *Suftine pro nunc* doth bend his brow,
And old crabb'd *Scotus*, on th' *Organon*,
Pay'th me with fnaphaunce, quick diftinction;
Habits, that intellectuall tearmed be,
Are got, or elfe infus'd from Deitie.
Dull Sorbonift, fly contradiction.
Fie, thou oppugn'ft the definition,
If one fhould fay; *Of things tearm'd rationall,*
Some reafon haue, others more fenfuall:
Would not fome frefhman, reading *Porphirie,*
Hiffe and deride fuch blockifh foolery?
Then vice nor vertue haue from habite place:
The one from want, the other facred grace,
Infus'd, difplac't, not in our will or force,
Bnt as it pleafe Iehoua *haue remorfe.*
I will, cries *Zeno:* O prefumption!
I can: thou maift, dogged opinion
Of thwarting Cynicks. To day vitious,
Lift to their percepts, next day vertuous.
Peace *Seneca,* thou belcheft blafphemy.
To liue from God, but to liue happily
(I heare thee boaft) *from thy Philofophy,*
And from thy felfe, O rauening lunacy!

                                          Cynicks,

Cynicks, yee wound your felues.   For Deftiny,
Ineuitable Fate, Neceffitie
You hold doth fway the acts fpirituall,
As well as parts of that wee mortall call.
Wher's then *I will?* wher's that ftrong Deity,
You do afcribe to your Philofophy?
Confounded Natures brats, can *will* and *Fate*
Haue both their feate, and office in your pate?
O hidden depth of that dread Secrecie,
Which I doe trembling touch in poetry!
To day, to day, implore obfequioufly:
Truft not *to morrowes will*; leaft vtterly
Yee be attach't with fad confuffon,
In your Grace-tempting lewd prefumption.
  But I forget: why fweat I out my braine,
In deep deffignes, to gay boyes, lewd, and vaine?
Thefe notes, were better fung, 'mong better fort:
But, to my pamphlet, few, faue fooles, refort.

Libri primi finis.

R 2   I cannot

PROEMIUM

IN

LIBRUM SECUNDUM.

I Cannot quote a motte Italionate,
 Or brand my Satyres with some Spanish terme,
I cannot with swolne lines magnificate
 Mine owne poore worth, or as immaculate
Taske others rimes; as if no blot did staine,
No blemish soyle my young Satyrick vaine.

Nor can I make my soule a merchandize,
 Seeking conceits to sute these Artlesse times,
Or daine for base reward to poetize:
 Soothing the world, with oyly flatteries.
Shall mercenary thoughts prouoke me write?
Shall I, for lucre, be a Parasite?

Shall I once pen for vulgar sorts applause?
 To please each hound? each dungy Scauenger?
To fit some Oyster-wenches yawning iawes?
 With tricksey tales of speaking Cornish dawes?
First let my braine (bright hair'd *Latonas* sonne)
Be cleane distract with all confusion.

What

What though some *Iohn-à-ftile* wilt bafely toyle,
   Only incited with the hope of gaine :
Though roguie thoughts do force some iade-like Moile;
   Yet no such filth my trae-borne Mufe will foyle.
O *Epictetus*, I doe honour thee,
To thinke how rich thou wert in pouertie.

<hr/>

Ad rithmum.

COme prettie pleafing fymphonie of words,
   Ye wel-matcht twins (whofe like-tun'd tongs affords
Such muficall delight) come willingly
And daunce *Leuoltoes* in my poefie.
Come all as eafie, as fpruce *Curio* will,
In fome Courthall, to fhew his capring fkill,
As willingly come meete and iump together,
As new ioyn'd loues, when they do clip each other.
As willingly, as wenches trip a round,
About a May-pole, after bagpipes found.
Come riming numbers, come and grace conceite,
Adding a pleafing clofe; with your deceipt,
Inticing eares.   Let not my ruder hand
Seeme once to force you in my lines to ftand.
Be not fo fearefull (prettie foules) to meete,
As *Flaccus* is, the Sergeants face to greete.
Be not fo backward, loth to grace my fenfe,
As *Drufus* is, to haue intelligence
His Dad's aliue; but come into my head
As iocundly, as (when his wife was dead)

R 3   Young

Young *Lelius* to his home. Come like-fac't rime,
In tunefull numbers keeping musicks time.
But if you hang an arse, like *Tubered*,
When *Chremes* dragd him from his brothell bed,
Then hence base ballad stuffe: my poetry
Disclaimes you quite. For know, my libertie
Scornes riming lawes. Alas poore idle sound :
Since I first *Phœbus* knew, I neuer found
Thy interest in sacred poesie.
Thou to Inuention add'st but surquedry,
A gaudie ornature : but hast no part,
In that soule-pleasing high infused art,
Then if thou wilt clip kindly in my lines,
Welcome thou friendly aide of my designes.
If not ? No title of my senselesse change
To wrest some forced rime, but freely range.
     Yee scrupulous obseruers, goe and Learne
     Of *Æsops* dogge; meat from a shade discerne.

✸✸✸✸✸✸✸✸✸✸ ✸ ✸✸✸✸✸✸✸✸✸✸

S A T Y R E V.

Totum in toto.

HAng thy selfe *Drusus:* hast nor armes nor braine ?
Some Sophy say, *The Gods sell all for paine.*
          Not so.
Had not that toyling Thebans steeled back
Dread poysoned shafts, liu'd he now, he should lack,
Spight of his farming Oxe-stawles. *Themis* selfe
Would be casheir'd from one poore scrap of pelse.

If

If that ſhe were incarnate in our time,
She might luſke ſcorned in diſdained ſlime,
Shaded from honour by ſome ennious miſt
Of watry fogges, that fill the ill-ſtuft liſt
Of faire Deſert, iealous euen of blind dark,
Leaſt it ſhould ſpie, and at their lameneſſe barke.
Honors ſhade thruſts honors ſubſtance from his place.
Tis ſtrange, when ſhade the ſubſtance can diſgrace.
Harſh lines cries *Curus*, whoſe eaues neïe reioyce,
But as the quauering of my Ladies voice.
Rude limping lines fits this lewd halting age.
Sweet ſenting *Curus*, pardon then my rage,
When wiſards ſweare plaine vertue neuer thriues:
None but *Priapus* by plaine dealing wiues.
Thou ſubtile *Hermes*, are the Deſtinies
Enamour'd on thee? then vp mount the ſkies.
Aduance, depoſe, do euen what thou liſt,
So long as Fates doe grace thy iuggling fiſt.
Tuſcus, haſt *Beuclarkes* armes and ſtrong ſinewes,
Large reach, full-fed vaines, ample reuenewes?
Then make thy markets by thy proper arme,
O, brawny ſtrength is an all-canning charme.
Thou dreadleſſe *Thracian*, haſt *Hallerbotius* ſlaine?
What? iſt not poſſible thy cauſe maintaine,
Before the dozen *Areopagites?*
Come *Enagonian*, furniſh him with ſlights,
Tut, *Plutos* wrath, *Proſerpina* can melt,
So that thy ſacrifice be freely felt.
What cannot *Iuno* force in bed with *Ioue?*
Turne and returne a ſentence with her loue,
Thou art too duſky. Fie, thou ſhallow Aſſe,
Put on more eyes, and marke me as I paſſe.

                                        Well

Well plainely thus; *Sleight, Force are mighty things,*
From which, much (if not most) earths glory springs
If vertues selfe, were clad in humane shape,
Vertue without these, might goe beg and scrape.
The naked truth is, a well-cloathed lie,
A nimble quick pate mounts to dignitie.
By force or fraude that matters not a jot;
So massie wealth may fall unto thy lot.

  I heard old *Albius* sweare, *Flavus* should haue
His eldeſt gurle, for *Flavus* was a knaue:
A damn'd deep-reaching villain, and would mount:
(He durſt well warrant him) to great account.
What though he laid forth all his ſtock and ſtore
Vpon ſome office, yet he'le gaine much more,
Though purchaſt deere. Tut, he will trebble it
In ſome fewe Termes, by his extorting wit.

  When I, in ſimple meaning, went to ſue
For tong-tide *Damus,* that would needs go wooe,
I prais'd him for his vertuous honeſt life.
By God, cryes *Flora,* Ile not be his wife.
He'le nere come on. Now I ſwear ſolemnely,
When I goe next, I'le praiſe his villany :
A better field to range in now a daies.
If vice be vertue, I can all men praiſe.

  What though pale *Maurus* paid huge ſymonies
For his halfe-dozen gelded vicaries :
Yet with good honeſt cut-throat vſury,
I feare he'le mount to reuerent dignity.
O ſleight! all-cunning ſleight! all-damning ſleight!
The onely gally-ladder unto might.

  Tuſcus is trade falſe : yet great hope he'le riſe,
For now he makes no count of periuries.

Hath

Hath drawn falfe lights from pitch-black loneries
Glafed his braided ware, cogs, fweares, and lies.
Now fince he hath the grace, thus gracelefle be,
His neighbours fweare, he'le fwell with treafurie.
Tut: Who maintaines, fuch goods, ill got, decay?
No: they'le fticke by the foule, they'le nerè away.
Lufcus, my Lords perfumer, had no fale,
Vntill he made his wife a brothell ftale.
Abfurd, the gods fell all for induftry?
When, what's not got by hell-bred villany?

  Codrus my well-fac't Ladies taile-bearer,
(He that fome-times play th' *Flauias* vfherer)
I heard one day complaine to *Lynceus,*
How vigilant, how right obfequious,
Modeft in carriage, how true in truft,
And yet (alas) nere guerdond with a cruft.
But now I fee, he findes by his accounts,
That fole Priapus, *by plaine dealing, mounts.*
How now? what, droupes the newe *Pegafian* Inne?
I feare mine hoft is honeft. Tut, beginne
To fet vp whorehoufe. Nere too late to thriue,
By any meanes, at *Porta Rich* arriue;
Goe vfe fome fleight, or liue poore *Irus* life,
Straight proftitute thy daughter, or thy wife;
And foone be wealthy: but be damn'd with it.
Hath not rich *Mylo* then deepe reaching wit?

Faire age!

When tis a high, and hard thing t'haue repute
Of a compleat villaine, perfect, abfolute,
And roguing vertue brings a man defame,
A packftaffe Epethite, and fcorned name.

Fie:

Fie; how my wit flagges! how heauily,
Me thinks I vent dull spriteleſſe poeſie!
What cold black froſt congeales my nummed brain?
What enuious power ſtops a Satyres vaine?
O now I knowe, the iuggling God of ſleights,
With *Caduceus* nimble *Hermes* fights,
And miſts my wit; offended, that my rimes
Diſplay his odious, world-abuſing crimes.
   O be propitious, powerfull God of Arts,
I ſheath my weapons, and do break my darts.
Be then appeas'd, Ile offer to thy ſhrine,
An *Hecatombe*, of many ſpotted kine.
Myriades of beaſts ſhall ſatisfie thy rage,
Which doe prophane thee in this Apiſh age.
   Infectious bloud, yée gouty humors quake,
   Whilſt my ſharpe Razor doth inciſion make.

❖❖❖❖❖❖❖❖❖❖❖❖❖❖❖❖❖❖❖❖❖❖❖❖❖

SATYRE VI.

Hem noſti'n.

C*Vrio,* know'ſt me? why thou bottle-ale,
   Thou barmie froth! O ſtay me leaſt I raile
Beyond *Nil vltra*; to ſee this butterfly,
This windy bubble taſke my balladry,
With ſenſeleſſe cenſure, *Curio,* know'ſt my ſp'rite?
Yet deem'ſt that in ſad ſeriouſneſſe I write?
Such naſty ſtuffe, as is *Pigmalion?*
Such maggot-tainted, lewd corruption.

Ha, how he glauers with his fawning fnowt,
And fweares, he thought, I meant but faintly flowt
My fine fmug rime, O barbarous dropfie noule!
Think'ft thou, that *Genius* that attends my foule,
And guides my fift to fcourge *Magnificoes*,
Wil daigne my minde be rank't in *Paphian* fhowes?
Thinkft thou, that I, which was create to whip
Incarnate fiends, will once vouchfafe to trip
A Paunis trauerfe? or will lifpe *(fweet loue)*
Or pule *(Aye me)* fome female foule to moue?
Think'ft thou, that I in melting poefie
Will pamper itching fenfualitie?
(That in the bodies fcumme all fatally
Intombes the foules moft facred faculty.)
    Hence thou misiudging Cenfor : know I wrot,
Thofe idle rimes, to note the odious fpot
And blemifh, that deformes the lineaments
Of moderne Poefies habiliments.
Oh that the beauties of inuention,
For want of iudgements difpofition,
Should all be fpoil'd.   O that fuch treafurie,
Such ftraines of well-conceited poefie,
Should moulded be, in fuch a fhapeleffe forme,
That want of Art fhould make fuch wit a fcorne.
    Here's one muft innocate fome lofe-leg'd Dame,
Some brothel drab, to helpe him ftanzaes frame,
Or els (alas) his wits can haue no vent,
To broch conceits induftrious intent.
Another yet dares tremblingly come out:
But firft he muft invoke good *Colin Clout.*
    Yon's one hath yean'd a fearefull prodigy,
Some monftrous misfhapen Balladry,

                                                His

His guts are in his braines, huge Iobbernoule,
Right Gurnets-head, the reft without all foule.
Another walkes, is lazie, lies him downe,
Thinkes, reades, at length fome wonted flepe doth crowne
His new falne lids, dreames, ftraight, ten pound to one,
Out fteps fome Fayery with quick motion,
And tells him wonders of fome flowry vale,
Awakes, ftraight rubs his eyes, and prints his tale.

    Yon's one, whofe ftraines haue flowne fo high a pitch,
That ftraight he flags, and tumbles in a ditch.
His fprightly hot high-foring poefie,
Is like that dreamed of Imagery,
Whofe head was gold, breft filuer, braffie thigh,
Lead Leggs, clay feete ; O faire fram'd poefie.

    Here's one, to get an vndeferu'd repute
Of deepe deepe learning, all in fuftian fute
Of ill paft, farre fetch't words attireth
His period, that all fenfe forfweareth.

    Another makes old *Homer Spencer* cite,
Like my *Pigmalion,* where, with rage, delight
He cryes, O *Ouid !* This caus'd my idle quill,
The world's dull eares with fuch lewd ftuff to fill,
And gull with bumbaft lines, the witleffe fenfe
Of thefe odde nags ; whofe pates circumference
Is fill'd with froth.   O thefe fame buzzing Gnats
That fting my fleeping browes ; thefe Nilus Rats,
Halfe dung, that haue their life from putrid flime,
Thefe that do praife my loofe lafciuious rime ;
For thefe fame fhades, I ferioufly proteft,
I flubberd vp that Chaos indigeft,
To fifh for fooles, that ftalke in goodly fhape:
What though in veluet cloake ? yet ftill an Ape.

Capre

Capro reads, fweares, fcrubs, and fweares againe,
Now by my foule an admirable ftraine,
Strokes vp his haire, cries paffing paffing good.
Oh, there's a line incends his luftfull blood.
   Then *Muto* comes, with his new glaffe-fet face,
And with his late kift-hand my booke doth grace,
Straight reades, then fmiles, and lifps *(tis pretty good)*
And praifeth that he neuer vnderftood.
But roome for *Flaccus,* he'le my Satyres read.
Oh how I trembled ftraight with inward dread!
But when I fawe him read my fuftian,
And heard him fweare I was a Pythian,
Yet ftraight recald, and fweares I did but quote
Out of *Xilinum* to that margents note;
I could fcarce hold, and keepe my felfe conceal'd,
But had well-nigh myfelfe and all reueal'd.
Then ftraight comes *Frifcus,* that neat Gentleman,
That newe difcarded Academian,
Who for he could cry *Ergo,* in the fchoole,
Straight-way, with his huge iudgment dares controule
Whatfo'ere he viewes; *That's prety good:*
That Epithite hath not that fprightly blood
Which fhould enforce it fpeake: that's Perfius *vaine:*
That's Iuvenal's, *heere'*s Horace *crabbld ftraine*:
Though he nere read one line in *Iuvenall,*
Or, in his life, his lazie eye let fall
On dufkie *Perfius.* O indignitie
To my refpectleffe free-bred poefie.
   Hence ye big-buzzing little-bodied Gnats,
Yee tatling Ecchoes, huge tongu'd Pigmy brats:
I meane to fleepe: wake not my flumbring braine,
With your malignant, weake, detracting vaine.
                    S   What

What though the sacred issue of my soule
I here expose to Idiots controule?
What though I beare, to lewd Opinion,
Lay ope, to vulgar prophanation,
My very *Genius?*   Yet know, my poesie
Doth scorne your vtmost, rank'st indignitie.
　My pate was great with child, and here tis eas'd
　Vexe all the world, so that thy selfe be pleas'd.

SATYRE VII.

A Cynicke Satyre.

A *Man, a man, a kingdome for a man.*
　Why how now currish, mad Athenian?
Thou Cynick dog, see'st not the streets do swarme
With troops of men? No, no: for *Cyrces* charme
Hath turn'd them all to Swine.   I neuer shall
Thinke those same *Samian* sawes authenticall:
But rather I dare sweare, the soules of swine
Doe liue in men.   For that same radiant shine,
That lustre wherewith natures *Nature* decked
Our intellectuall part, that glosse is soyled
With stayning spots of vile impiety,
And muddy durt of sensualitie.
These are no men, but *Apparitions,*
Ignes fatui, Glowewormes, Fictions,
Meteors, Rats of Nilus, Fantasies,
Colosses, Pictures, Shades, Resemblances.
　　　　Ho *Linceus!*

　　　　　　　　　　　　　　　　Seest thou

Seeſt thou yon gallant in the ſumptuous clothes,
How briſk, how ſpruce, how gorgiouſly he ſhews?
Note his French-herring bones: but note no more,
Vnleſſe thou ſpy his faire appendant where,
That lackies him.   Marke nothing but his clothes,
His new ſtampt complement, his Cannon oathes.
Marke thoſe: for naught, but ſuch lewd vicioufnes,
Ere graced him, ſaue Sodome beaſtlineſſe.
Is this a *Man?* Nay, an incarnate deuill,
That ſtruts in vice, and glorioth in euill.

   A man, a man.. Peace Cynick, yon is one:
A compleat ſoule of all perfection.
What, mean'ſt thou him that walks all open breſted?
Drawn through the eare with Ribands, plumy creſte.
He that doth ſnort in fat-fed luxury,
And gapes for ſome grinding Monopoly?
He that in effeminate inuention,
In beaſtly ſource of all pollution,
In ryot, luſt, and fleſhly ſeeming ſweetneſſe,
Sleepes ſound ſecure, under the ſhade of greatneſſe?
Mean'ſt thou that ſenceleſſe, ſenſuall Epicure?
That ſinke of filth, that guzzle moſt impure?
What he? *Linceus* on my word thus preſume,
He's nought but clothes, and ſenting ſweet perfume.
His verie ſoule, aſſure thee *Linceus,*
Is not ſo bigge as is an Atomus:
Nay, he is ſprightleſſe, ſenſe or ſoule hath none,
Since laſt *Meduſa* turn'd him to a ſtone.

   A man, a man; Lo yonder I eſpie
The ſhade of *Neſtor* in ſad grauitie.
Since old *Sylenus* brake his Aſſes back,
He now is forc't his paunch, and guts to pack

In a

In a faire Tumbrell.   Why, fower Satyrift,
Canft thou vnman him ? Here I dare infift
And foothly fay, he is a perfect foule,
Eates Nectar, drinkes Ambrofia, faunce controule.
An inundation of felicitie
Fats him with honor, and huge treafurie.
Canft thou not *Linceus* caft thy fearching eye,
And fpy his eminent Cataftrophe?
He's but a fpunge, and fhortly needes muft leefe
His wrong got iuice, when greatnes fift fhall fqueefe
His liquor out.   Would not fome head,
That is with feeming fhadowes only fed,
Sweare yon fame Damafke-coat, yon garded man
Were fome graue fober *Cato Vtican?*
When let him but in iudgements fight vncafe,
He's naught but budge, old gards, browne fox-fur face
He hath no foule, the which the Stagerite
Term'd rationall: for beaftly appetite,
Bafe dunghill thoughts, and fenfuall action
Hath made him loofe that faire creation.
And now no man, fince *Circes* magick charme
Hath turn'd him to a maggot, that doth fwarme
In tainted flefh: whofe foule corruption
Is his faire foode: whofe generation
Anothers ruine.   O *Canaans* dread curfe
To liue in peoples finnes.   Nay far more worfe
To muke ranke hate.   But firra, *Linceus,*
Seeft thou that troupe that now affronteth vs?
They are nought but Eeles, that neuer will appeare
Till that tempeftuous winds or thunder teare
Their flimy beds.   But prithee ftay a while,
Looke, yon comes *Iohn-a-noke*, and *Iohn-a-ftile,*

They are

They are nought but flowe-pac't, dilatory pleas,
Demure demurrers, ftil ftriuing to appeafe
Hote zealous loue.   The language that they fpeake,
Is the pure barbarous blackfaunt of the *Geate :*
Their only fkill refts in *Collufions,*
Abatements, ftoppels, inhibitions.
Heauy-pas't Iades, dull pated Iobernoules
Quick in delayes, checking with vaine controules
Faier Iuftice courfe, vile neceffary euils,
Smooth feeming-faints, yet damn'd incarnate diuels.

    Farre be it from my fharpe Satyrick Mufe,
Thofe graue and reuerend legifts to abufe,
That aide *Aftrea,* that doe further right :
But thefe *Megera's* that inflame defpight,
That broche deepe rancor, that do ftudy ftill
To ruine right, that they their panch may fill
With *Irus* bloud; thefe Furies I doe meane,
Thefe Hedge-hogs, that difturbe *Aftreas* Scean.

    A man, a man: peace Cynicke, yon's a man,
Behold yon fprightly dread *Mauortian*   -
With him I ftop thy currifh barking chops.
What, meanft thou him, that in his fwaggring flops
Wallowes vnbraced, all along the ftreete?
He that falutes each gallant he doth meete,
With *farewell fweete captaine, kind' hart, adew,*
He that laft night, tumbling thou didft view
From out the great mans head; and thinking ftill
He had beene Sentinell of warlike Brill,
Cryes out *Que va la?* zounds *Que?* and out doth draw
His transformd ponyard, to his *Syringe* ftraw,
And ftabs the drawer.   What, that *Ringo roote?*
Mean'ft thou that wafted leg, puffe bumbaft boot?

What, he

What, he that's drawne, and quartered with lace ?
That *Weſtphalian* gamon Cloue-ſtuck face ?
Why, he is nought but huge blaſpheming othes,
Swart ſnout, big looks, misſhapen Switzers clothes.
Weake meager luſt hath now conſumed quite,
And waſted cleane away his Martiall ſpright:
Infeebling ryot, all vices confluence
Hath eaten out that ſacred influence
Which made'him man.
That diuine part is ſoak't away in ſinne,
In ſenſuall luſt, and midnight bezeling,
Ranke inundation of luxuriouſneſſe
Haue tainted him with ſuch groſſe beaſtlineſſe,
That now the ſeat of that celeſtiall eſſence
Is all poſſeſt with Naples peſtilence.
Fat peace, and diſſolute impietie.
Haue lulled him in ſuch ſecuritie,
That now, let whirlwinds and confuſion teare:
The Center of our ſtate, let Giants reare
Hill upon hill, let weſterne *Termagant*
Shake heauens vault; he with his Occupant,
Are clingd ſo cloſe, like deaw-worms in the morne
That he'le not ſtir, till out his guts are torne
With eating filth. *Lubrio,* ſnort on, ſnort on,
Till thou art wak't with ſad confuſion.

    Now raile no more at my ſharpe Cynick ſound,
Thou brutiſh world, that in all yileneſſe drown'd
Haſt loſt thy ſoule: for naught but ſhades I ſee,
Reſemblances of men inhabite thee.
    Yon Tiſſue ſlop, yon Holy-croſſed pane,
Is but a water-ſpaniell that will faune,

                  And kiſſe.

And kiſſe the water, whilſt it pleaſures him:
But being once arriued at the brim,
He ſhakes it off.

Yon in the capring cloake, a mimick Ape,
That ouely ſtriues to ſeeme an others ſhape.

Yon's *Æſops* Aſſe, yon ſad ciuility
Is but an Oxe, that with baſe drudgery
Eates vp the land, whilſt ſome gilt Aſſe doth chaw
The golden wheat; he well apayd with ſtraw.

Yon's but a muckhill ouer-ſpred with ſnowe,
Which with that vaile doth euen as fairely ſhowe
As the greene meades, whoſe natiue outward faire
Breathes ſweet perfumes into the neighbour ayre.

Yon effeminate ſanguine *Ganimede,*
Is but a Beuer, hunted for the bed.

Peace Cynick, *ſee what yonder doth approach,*
A cart? a tumbrell? no, a badged coach.
What's in't? ſome man. *No, nor yet woman kinde,*
But a celeſtiall Angell, faire refinde.
The diuell as ſoone. Her maſke ſo hinders me
I cannot ſee her beauties deitie.
Now that is off, ſhe is ſo vizarded,
So ſteept in Lemons iuyce, ſo ſurphuled
I cannot ſee her face. Vnder one hoode
Two faces: but I neuer underſtood
Or ſaw one face vnder two hoods till now.
Tis the right ſemblance of old *Ianus* brow.
Her maſke, her vizard, her looſe-hanging gowne,
(For her looſe lying body) her bright ſpangled crowne
Her long ſlit ſleeues, ſtiffe buſke, puffe verdingall
Is all that makes her thus angelicall.

Alas, her

Alas, her foule ftruts round about her neck,
Her feate of fenfe is her rebato fet,
Her intellectuall is a fained niceneffe,
Nothing but clothes, and fimpring precifeneffe.
   Out on thefe puppets, painted Images,
Haberdafhers fhops, torch-light mafkeries,
Perfuming pans, Dutch ancients, Glowe-worms bright
That foyle our foules, and dampe our reafons light:
Away, away, hence Coach-man, goe infhrine
Thy new glas'd puppet in port Efqueline.
Blufh *Martia*, feare not, or looke pale, all's one,
Margara keepes thy fet complexion.
Sure I nere thinke thofe axioms to be true,
That foules of men, from that great foule enfue,
And of his effence doe participate
As 'twere by pipes; when fo degenerate,
So aduerfe is our natures motion,
To his immaculate condition:
That fuch foule filth, from fuch faire puritie,
Such fenfuall acts, from fuch a Deitie,
Can nere proceed.   But if that dreame were fo,
Then fure the flime, that from our foules do flowe,
Haue ftopt thofe pipes by which it was conuei'd,
And now no humane creatures; once diftai'd
Of that faire iem.
Beafts *fenfe*, plants *growth*, like being as a ftone.
But out alas, our *Cognifance* is gone.

Finis libri fecundi.

In ferious

PROEMIUM

IN

LIBRUM TERTIUM.

IN ferious ieft, and iefting ferioufneffe,
I ftriue to fcourge polluting beaftlineffe,
I inuocate no *Delian* Deitie,
Nor facred of-fpring of *Mnemofyne*:
I pray in aid of no *Caftalian* Mufe,
No Nymph, no femal Angell to infufe
A fprightly wit to raife my flagging wings,
And teach me tune thefe harfh difcordant ftrings.
I craue no Syrens of our Halcion times,
To grace the accents of my rough-hew'd rimes:
But grim *Reproofe*, ftearne hate of villany,
Infpire and guid a Satyres poefie
Faire *Deteftation* of foule odious finne,
In which our fwinifh times lye wallowing.
Be thou my conduct and my *Genius*,
My wits inciting fweet breath'd *Zephirus*.
O that a Satyres hand had force to pluck
Some fludgate vp, to purge the world from muck:
                                                Would God

Would God I could turne *Alpheus* riuer in,
To purge this *Augean* Oxftall from foule finne.
  Well, I will try: awake impuritie,
  And view the vaile drawne from thy villany.

* * *

S A T Y R E VIII.

Iamorato Curio.

*C*Vrio, aye me! thy miftreſ Monkey's dead,
  Alaſ, alas, her pleaſures burièd.
Goe woman's flaue, performe his exequies,
Condole his death in mournfull Elegies.
Tut, rather Peans fing *Hermaphrodite :*
For that fad death giues life to thy delight.
  Sweete fac't *Corinna,* daine.the riband tie
Of thy Cork-fhooe, or els thy flaue will die :
Some puling Sonnet toles his paffing bell,
Some fighing Elegie muft ring his knell,
Vnleffe bright funfhine of thy grace reuiue
His wambling ftomack, certes he will diue
Into the whirle-poole of deuouring death,
And to fome Mermaid facrifice his breath.
Then oh, *oh then,* to thy eternall fhame,
And to the honour of fweet *Curios* name,
This Epitaph, vpon the Marble ftone,
Muft faire be grau'd of that true louing one;

      Heere lyeth he, he lyeth here,
        That bouſc't and pittie cryed :
      The doore not op't, fell ficke alas,
        Alas fell ficke and dyed.

                              What Mirmidon

What Mirmidon, or hard Dolopian,
What fauage minded rude Cyclopian,
But fuch a fweete pathetique Paphian
Would force to laughter? Ho *Amphitrion,*
Thou art no Cuckold. What though *Ioue* dallied,
During thy warres, in faire *Alcmenas* bed,
Yet *Hercules* true borne, that imbecillitie
Of corrupt nature all apparantly
Appeares in him. O foule indignitie,
I heard him vow himfelfe a flaue to *Omphale,*
Puling *(aye me)* O valours obloquie!
He that the inmoft nookes of hell did know,
Whofe nere craz'd proweffe all did ouer-throw,
Lyes ftreaking brawny limmes in weakning bed,
Perfum'd, fmooth kemb'd, new glaz'd, fair furphuled:
O that the boundleffe power of the foule
Should be fubieƈted to fuch bafe controule!

   Big limm'd *Alcides,* doffe thy honours crowne,
Goe fpin, huge flaue, leaft *Omphale* fhould frowne.
By my beft hopes, I blufh with griefe and fhame
To broach the peafant bafeneffe of our name.

   O now my ruder hand begins to quake,
To thinke what loftie Cedars I muft fhake:
But if the canker fret the barkes of Oakes,
Like humbler fhrubs fhall equal beare the ftroaks
Of my refpeƈtleffe rude Satyrick hand.

   Vnleffe the Deftin's adamantine band
Should tye my teeth, I cannot chufe but bite,
To view *Mauortius* metamorphoz'd quite
To puling fighes, and into *(aye mee's)* ftate,
With voice diftinƈt, all fine articulate.

                                            Lifping,

Lifping, *Faire faint, my woe compaffionate:*
By heauen, thine eye is my foule-guiding fate.

    The God of wounds had wont on *Cyprian* couch
To ftreake himfelfe, and with incenfing touch
To faint his force, onely when wrath had end:
But now, 'mong furious garboiles, he doth fpend
His feebled valour, in tilt and turneying,
With wet turn'd kiffes, melting dallying.
A poxe vpon't, that *Bacchis* name fhould be
The watch-word giuen to the fouldierie.
Goe troupe to field, mount thy obfcured fame,
Cry out *S. George,* invoke thy miftreffe name;
Thy Miftreffe and *S. George,* alarum cry
Weake force, weake ayde, that fprouts from luxury.

    Thou tedious workmanfhip of luft-ftung *Ioue,*
Down from thy fkyes, enioy our females loue:
Some fiftie more *Beotian* girles will fue
To haue thy loue, fo that thy back be true.

    O now me thinks I heare fwart *Martius* cry,
Souping along in warres faind mafkerie,
By *Lais* ftarrie front he'le forth-with die
In cluttred bloud, his Miftres liuorie.
Her fancies colours waues vpon his head.
O well fenc't *Albion,* mainly manly fped,
When thofe, that are Soldadoes in thy ftate,
Doe beare the badge of bafe, effeminate,
Euen on their plumie crefts: brutes fenfuall,
Hauing no fparke of intellectual.
Alack, what hope? when fome rank nafty wench
Is fubiect of their vowes and confidence?
    Publius hates vainly to idolatries,
And laughes that papifts honour Images:

                          And yet

And yet (O madneſſe) theſe mine eyes did ſee
Him melt in mouing plants, obſequiouſly
Imploring fauor, twining his kinde armes,
Vſing inchauntments, exorciſmes, charmes.
The oyle of Sonnets, wanton blandiſhment,
The force of teares, and ſeeming languiſhment,
Vnto the picture of a painted laſſe:
I ſaw him court his Miſtreſſe looking-glaſſe,
Worſhip a buſk-point, which in ſecrecie
I feare was conſcious of ſtrange villany.
I ſaw him crouch, deuote his liuelihood,
Sweare, proteſt, vow peſant feruitude
Vnto a painted puppet, to her eyes
I heard him ſweare his ſighes to ſacrifice.
But if he get her itch-alaying pinne,
O ſacred relique, ſtraight he muſt beginne
To raue out-right: then thus; *Celeſtiall bliſſe,*
Can heauen grant ſo rich a grace as this?
Touch it not (by the Lord Sir) tis diuine,
It once beheld her radiant eyes bright ſhine:
Her haire imbrac't it, O thrice happy prick
That there was throu'd, and in her haire didſt ſtick.
Kiſſe, bleſſe, adore it *Publius*, neuer linne,
Some ſacred vertue lurketh in the pinne.
    O frantick fond pathetique paſſion!
Iſt poſſible ſuch ſenſuall action
Should clip the wings of contemplation?
O can it be the ſpirits function,
The ſoule, not ſubiect to dimenſion,
Should be made ſlaue to reprehenſion
Of crafty natures paint? Fie, can our ſoule
Be vnderling to ſuch a vile controule?
              T   *Saturio.*

Saturio wifh't himfelfe his Miftreffe bufke,
That he may fweetly lie, and foftly lufke
Betweene her paps, then muft he haue an eye
At eyther end, that freely might defcry
Both hils and dales.   But out on *Phrigio*,
That wifh't he were his Miftreffe dog, to goe
And licke her milke-white fift.   O pretty grace,
That pretty *Phrigio* begs but Pretties place.
Parthenophell, thy wifh I will omit,
So beaftly tis I may not vtter it.
But *Punicus*, of all I'le beare with thee,
That faine would'ft be thy miftreffe fmug munkey :
Here's one would be a flea, (ieft comicall)
Another his fweet Ladies verdingall,
To clip her tender breech : Another he
Her filuer-handled fan would gladly be :
Here's one would be his Miftreffe neck-lace faine,
To clip her faire, and kiffe her azure vaine.
Fond fooles, well wifht, and pitty but fhould be :
For beaftly fhape to brutifh foules agree.

  If *Lauras* painted lip doe daine a kiffe.
To her enamour'd flaue, *O heauens bliffe!*
(Straight he exclames) *not to be matcht with this!*
Blafpheming dolt, goe three-fcore fonnets write
Vpon a pictures kiffe, O rauing fpright!
  I am not fapleffe, old, or reumatick,
No *Hipponax* misfhapen ftigmatick,
That I fhould thus inueigh 'gainft amorous fpright
Of him whofe foule doth turne *Hermaphrodite :*
But I doe fadly grieue, and inly vexe,
To viewe the bafe difhonour of our fexe.
                              Tufh, guilt-

Tuſh, guiltleſſe Doues, when Gods to force foule rapes
Will turne themſelues to any brutiſh ſhapes.
Baſe baſtard powers, whom the world doth ſee
Transform'd to ſwine for ſenſuall luxurie.
The ſonne of *Saturne* is become a Bull,
To crop the beauties of ſome female trull.
Now, when he hath his firſt wife *Metim* ſped,
And fairely clok't, leaſt foole gods ſhould be bred
Of that fond Mule: *Themis* his ſecond wife
Hath turn'd away, that his vnbrideled life
Might haue more ſcope. Yet laſt his ſiſters loue
Muſt ſatiate the luſtfull thoughts of *Ioue*.
Now doth the lecher in a Cuckowes ſhape
Commit a monſtrous and inceſtuous rape.
Thrice ſacred gods, and O thrice bleſſed ſkies,
Whoſe orbes includes ſuch vertuous deities.
What ſhould I ſay? Luſt hath confounded all.
The bright gloſſe of our intellectuall
Is fouly ſoyl'd. The wanton wallowing
In fond delights, and amorous dallying.
Hath duſk't the faireſt ſplendour of our ſoule:
Nothing now left, but carkas, lothſome, foule.
For ſure, if that ſome ſpright remained ſtill,
Could it be ſubiect to lewd *Lais* will?

Reaſon by prudence in her function
Had wont to tutor all our action,
Ayding with precepts of philoſophie
Our feebled natures imbecillitie:
But now affection, will, concupiſcence
Haue got o're Reaſon chiefe preheminence
Tis ſo: els how ſhould ſuch vile baſeneſſe taint
As force it be made ſlaue to natures paint?

T 2   Me thinks

Me thinks the fpirits Pegafe *Fantafie*
Should hoyfe the foule from fuch bafe flauery:
But now I fee, and can right plainly fhowe
From whence fuch abioct thoughts and actions grow.
　Our aduerfe bodie, being earthly, cold,
Heauie, dull, mortall, would not long infold
A ftranger inmate, that was backward ftill
To all his dungy, brutifh, fenfuall will:
Now here-vpon, our 'Intellectuall,
Compact of fire all celeftiall,
Invifible, immortall, and diuine,
Grew ftraight to fcorn his land-lords muddy flime:
And therefore now is clofely flunke away
(Leauing his fmoaky houfe of mortall clay)
Adorn'd with all his beauties lineaments
And brighteft iems of fhining ornaments,
His parts diuine, facred, fpirituall,
Attending on him; leauing the fenfuall
Bafe hangers on, lufking at home in flime,
Such as wont to ftop port Efqueline.
Now doth the bodie, led with fenfeleffe will,
(The which in reafons abfence ruleth ftill)
Raue, talke idely, as t'were fome deitie
Adorning female painted puppetry,
Playing at put-pin, doting on fome glaffe
(Which breath'd but on, his falfed gloffe doth paffe)
Toying with babies and with fond paftime,
Some childrens fporte, deflowring of chafte time,
Imploying all his wits in vaine expenfe,
Abufing all his organons of fenfe.
　Returne, returne, facred *Synderefis*,
Infpire our trunks: let not fuch mud as this

　　　　　　　　　　　　　Pollute

Pollute vs ftill: Awake our lethargy,
Raife vs from out our brain-ficke foolery.

✳✳✳✳✳✳✳✳✳✳ ✳ ✳✳✳✳✳✳✳✳✳✳

·SATYRE IX.

Here's a toy to mocke an Ape indeede.

GRim-fac't *Reproofe*, fparkle with threatning eye,
  Bend thy fower browes in my tart poefie.
Auaunt yee curres, houle in fome cloudy mift,
Quake to behold a fharp-fangd Satyrift.
O how on tip-toes proudly mounts my Mufe!
Stalking a loftier gate then Satyres vfe.
Me thinks fome facred rage warmes all my vaines,
Making my fpright mount vp to higher ftraines
Then well befeemes a rough-tongu'd Satyres part:
But Art curbs Nature, Nature guideth Art.

  Come downe yee Apes, or I will ftrip you quite,
Baring your bald tayles to the peoples fight.
Yee mimick flaues, what are you percht fo hie?
Downe Iack an Apes from thy fain'd royalty.
What furr'd with beard, caft in a Satin fute,
Iudiciall Tack? how haft thou got repute
Of a found cenfure?   O idiot times,
When gaudy Monkeys mowe ore fprightly rimes!
O world of fooles, when all mens indgement's fet,
And reft vpon fome mumping Marmofet!
Yon Athens Ape (that can but fimpringly
Yaule *Auditores humaniffimi,*

                T 3   Bound

Bound to fome feruile imitation,
Can with much fweat patch an oration)
Now vp he comes, and with his crooked eye
Prefumes to fquint on fome faire Poefie;
And all as thankleffe as ungratefull Thames
He flinks away, leauing but reaking fteames
Of dungy flime behinde.   All as ingrate
He vfeth it, as when I fatiate
My fpanielles paunch, who ftraight perfumes the roome,
With his tailes filth: fo this vnciuill groome,
Ill-tutor'd pedant, *Mortimers* numbers
With much-pit Efculine filth befcumbers.
Now th'Ape chatters, and is as malecontent
As a bill-patch't doore, whofe entrailes out haue fent
And fpewd their tenant.
　　My foule adores iudiciall fchollerfhip:
But when to feruile imitatorfhip
Some fpruce Athenian pen is prentized,
Tis worfe then Apifh.   Fie, be not flattered
With feeming worth.   Fond affectation
Befits an Ape, and mumping Babilon.
O what a trickfie lerned nicking ftrain
Is this applauded, fenfeleffe, modern † vain!
When late I heard it from fage *Mutius* lips
How ill me thought fuch wanton liggin fkips
Befeem'd his grauer fpeech.   *Farre fly thy fame*
Moft, moft, of me beloued, whofe filent name
One letter bounds.   Thy true iudiciall ftile
I euer honour: and if my loue beguilt

---

† *Non lædere, fed ludere: non lanea, fed linea: non*
ictus, fed nictus potius.

Not much

Not much my hopes, then thy enualued worth
Shall mount faire place, when Apes are turned forth.

   I am too mild: reach me my fcourge againe.
O yon's a pen fpeakes in a learned vaine,
Deepe, paft all fenfe. Lanthorne and candle light,
Here's all inuifible, *all mentall fpright.*
What hotch potch, giberidge doth the Poet bring?
How ftrangely fpeakes? yet fweetly doth he fing.
I once did know a tinkling Pewterer,
That was the vileft ftumbling ftutterer
That euer hack't and hew'd our natiue tongue:
Yet to the Lute if you had heard him fung,
Iefu how fweet he breath'd! You can apply.
O fenfeleffe profe, iudiciall poefie,
How ill you'r link't. This affectation,
To fpeake beyond mens apprehenfion,
How Apifh tis! When all in fuftian fute
Is cloth'd a huge *nothing,* all for repute
Of profound knowledge, when profoundnefs knowes
There's naught contain'd, but onely feeming fhowes.
   O! Iack of Paris-garden, canft thou get
A faire rich fute, though fouly run in debt?
Looke fmug, fmell fweet, take vp commodities,
Keepe whores, fee bauds, belch impious blafphemies,
Wallow along in fwaggering difguife,
Snuffe vp fmoak-whiffs, and each morne 'fore fhe rife,
Vifit thy drab? Canft vfe a falfe cut die
With a cleane grace, and glib facilitie?
Canft thunder cannon oathes, like th'rattling
Of a huge, double, ful-charg'd culuering?
Then Iack troupe 'mong our gallants, kiffe thy fift,
And call them brothers: Say a Satyrift

Sweares

Sweares they are thine in neere affinitie,
All coosin germanes, faue in villany.
For (fadly truth to fay) what are they elfe
But imitators of lewd beaftlyneffe?
Farre worfe than Apes; for mowe, or fcratch your pate,
It may be fome odde Ape will imitate :
But let a youth that hath abus'd his time,
In wronged trauaile, in that hoter clime,
Swoope by old Iack, in cloathes Italionate:
And I'le be hang'd if he will imitate.
His ftrange fantaftique fute fhapes :
Or let him bring or'e beaftly luxuries,
Some hell-deuifed luftfull villanies,
Euen Apes and beafts would blufh with natiue fhame;
And thinke it foule difhonour to their name,
Their beaftly name, to imitate fuch finne·
As our lewd youths doe boaft and glory in.
  Fie, whether do thefe Monkeys carry mee?
Their very names do foyle my poefie.
Thou world of Marmofets and mumping Apes,
Vnmaſke, put off thy fained borrowed fhapes,
Why lookes neat *Curus* all fo fimpringly?
Why babbleft thou of deepe Diuinitie?
And of that facred teftimoniall?
Liuing voluptuous like a *Bacchanall?*
Good hath thy tongue: but thou rank Puritan;
I'le make an Ape as good a Chriftian.
I'le force him chatter, turning vp his eye,
Looke fad, go graue. Demure ciuilitie
Shall feeme to fay, *Good brother, fifter deers.*
As for the reft, to fnort in belly cheere,

                                        To bite

To bite, to gnaw, and boldly intermell
With facred things, in which thou doſt excell,
Vnforc't he'le doe.   O take compaſſion
Euen on your foules: make not religion
A bawde to lewdneſſe.   Civill *Socrates*
Clyp not the youth of *Alcibiades*
With unchaſt armes.   Difguifed *Meſſaline*
I'le teare thy maſke, and bare thee to the eyne
Of hiſſing boyes, if to the Theatres
I finde thee once more come for lecherers,
To fatiate (nay, to tyer) thee with the vfe
Of weakning luſt.   Yee fainers, leaue t'abufe
Our better thoughts with your hypocrifie:
Or by the euer-liuing veritie,
I'le ſtrip you nak't, and whip you with my rimes,
Cauſing your ſhame to liue to after-times.

✿✱✿✱✿✱✿✱✿✱✿✱✿✱✿✱✿✱✿✱✿✱✿✱✿✱✿✱✿

S A T Y R E X.

Stultorum plena funt omnia.

To his very friend, Maſter E. G.

FRom out the fadneſſe of my difcontent,
    Hating my wonted iocund merriment,
(Only to giue dull time a fwifter wing)
Thus fcorning fcorne, of Idiot fooles I fing.
I dread no bending of an angry brow,
Or rage of fooles that I ſhall purchafe now.

                                        Who'le

Who'le scorn to sit in ranke of foolery,
When I'le be maister of the company?
For pre-thee *Ned*, I pre-thee gentle lad,
Is not he frantique, foolish, bedlam mad,
That wastes his spright, that melts his very braine
In deepe designes, in wits dark gloomy straine?
That scourgeth great slaues with a dreadlesse fist,
Playing the rough part of a Satyrist,
To be perus'd by all the dung-scum rable
Of thin-braind Idiots, dull, vncapable?
For mimicke apish schollers, pedants, guls,
Perfmu'd inamoratoes, brothell truls?
Whilst I (poore soule) abuse chast virgin time,
Deflowring her with unconceiued rime.
Tut, tut, a toy of an idle empty braine,
Some scurril iests, light gew-gawes, fruitlesse, vaine.
Cryes beard-graue *Dromus*, when alas, god knows
His toothlesse gum nere chew but outward shows.
Poore budge face, bowcase sleeue, but let him passe
Once furre and beard shall priuiledge an Asse.

And tell me *Ned*, what might that gallant be,
Who to obtaine intemperate luxury,
·Cuckolds his elder brother, gets an heire,
By which his hope is turned to despaire?
In faith (good *Ned)* he damn'd himselfe with cost:
For well thou know'st full goodly land was lost.

I am too priuate,   *Yet me thinkes an Asse*
Rimes well with V I D E R I T V T I L I T A S.
Euen full as well, I boldly dare auerre
As any of that stinking Scauenger
Which from his dunghill he bedaubed on
The latter page of old *Pigmalion.*

                                        O that

O that this brother of hypocrifie
(Applauded by his pure fraternitie)
Should thus be puffed, and fo proude infift,
As play on me the Epigrammatift.
Opinion mounts this froth vnto the fkies,
Whom iudgemente reafon iuftly vilifies.
For (fhame to the Poet) reade *Ned*, behold
How wittily a Maifters-hoode can fcold.

An Epigram which the Author *Vergidemiarum*, caufed to
be pafted to the latter page of euery *Pigmalion*, that
came to the Stationers of Cambridge.

I Afk't Phifitions what their counfell was
For a mad dogge, or for a mankind Affe?
They told me though there were confections ftore
Of Poppie-feede, and foueraigne Hellebore,
The dogge was beft cured by cutting and ‡ kinfing,
The Affe muft be kindly whipped for winfing.
Now then S. K. I little paffe
Whether thou be a mad dogge, or a mankind Affe.

Medice cura teipfum.

Smart ierke of wit! Did ever fuch a ftraine
Rife from an Apifh fchoole-boyes childifh braine?
Doft thou not blufh good *Ned*, that fuch a fent
Should rife from thence where thou hadft nutriment?
Shame to Opinion, that perfumes his dung,
And ftreweth flowers rotten bones among.
Iuggling Opinion, thou inchaunting witch,
Paint not a rotten poft with colours rich.

---

‡ *Mark the witty allufion to my name.*

But now

But now this iuggler with the worlds consent
Hath half his soule; the other, Complement,
Mad world the whilst. But I forget mee, I,
I am seduced with this poesie:
And madder then a Bedlam spend sweet time
In bitter numbers, in this idle rime.
Out on this humour. From a sickly bed,
And from a moodie minde distempered,
I vomit forth my loue, now turn'd to hate,
Scorning the honour of a Poets state.
Nor shall the kennell rout of muddy braines
Rauish my Muses heyre, or hoare my straines,
Once more. No nittie pedant shall correct
Ænigmaes to his shallow intellect.
Inchauntment *Ned* hath rauished my sense
In a Poetick vaine circumference.
Yet thus I hope (God shield I now should lie)
Many more fooles, and most more wise then I.

V.A.L.E.

❀❀❀❀❀❀❀❀ ❀❀❀❀❀❀❀❀

S A T Y R E XI.

Humours.

SLeep grim *Reproofe:* my iocund Muse doth sing
In other keys, to nimbler fingering.
Dull sprighted *Melancholy*, leaue my brain
To hell *Cimerian* night, in liuely vaine
I striue to paint, then hence all darke intent
And sullen frownes: come sporting merriment,

Cheeke

Cheeke dimpling laughter, crowne my very foule
With iouifance, whilſt mirthfull iefts controule
The gouty humours of theſe pride-ſwolne daies,
Which I do long vntill my pen diſplaies.
O I am great with mirth: ſome midwifrie,
Or I ſhall breake my ſides ſo vanitie.
Roome for a capering mouth, whoſe lips nere ſtur,
But in difcourſing of the gracefull ſtur.
Who euer heard ſpruce ſkipping *Curio*
Ere prate of ought, but of the whirle on toe,
The name about ground, *Robrus* ſprauling kicks,
Fabius caper, *Harries* toffing tricks?
Did euer any eare ere heare him fpeake
Vnleſſe his tongue of croſſe-points did intreat?
His teeth doe caper whilſt he eates his meat,
His heeles doe caper, whilſt he takes his ſeate,
His very ſoule, his intellectuall
Is nothing but a mincing capreall.
He dreames of toe-turnes, each gallant he doth meete
He fronts him with a trauerfe in the ſtreete.
Praiſe but *Orcheſtra*, and the ſkipping Art,
You ſhall commaund him, faith you haue his hart.
Euen capring in your fift. A hall, a hall,
Roome for the Spheres, the orbs celeſtiall.
Will daunce *Kemps Iigge*. They'le reuel with neate iumps.
A worthy Poet hath put on their Pumps.
O wits quick trauerſe, but ſhadowe's flowe,
Good faith tis hard for nimble *Curio*,
Ye gracious Orbes, keepe the old meaſuring,
All's ſpoilde if once yee fall to caping.
   Luſcus what's plaid to day? faith now I know
I ſet thy lips abroach, from whence doth flowe

U   Naught

Naught but pure *Iuliet* and *Romeo*.
Say who acts best? *Drusus* or *Roscio?*
Now I haue him, that nere of ought did speake
But when of playes or Players he did treat.
Hath made a common-place booke out of playes,
And speakes in print: at least what ere he saies
Is warranted by Curtaine *plaudities,*
If ere you heard him courting *Lesbias* eyes;
Say (Curteous Sir) speakes he not mouingly,
From out some new pathetique Tragedy?
He writes, he railes, he iests, he courts, (what not?)
And all from out his huge long scraped stock
Of well penn'd playes.

 Oh come not within distance: *Martius* speakes,
Who nere discourseth but of fencing feats,
Of *counter times, sinctures,* sly *passataes,*
Stramazones, resolute *Stoccates,*
Of the quick change with wiping *mandritta,*
The *carricado,* with th' *enbrocata,*
Ob, by Iesu sir (me thinks I heare him cry)
The honourable fencing mystery
Who doth not honour? Then fals he in againe,
Lading our eares, and somewhat must be saine
Of blades, and Rapier-hilts, of surest garde,
Of *Vincentio,* and the *Burgonians* ward.

 This bumbast foile-button I once did see
By chaunce, in *Linias* modest company,
When after the *God-sauing* ceremony,
For want of talke-stuffe, fals to foinery,
Out goes his Rapier, and to *Liuia*
He shewes the ward by *puncta reuersa,*
         The incauata.

The *incarnata.* Nay, by the bleſſed light,
Before he goes, he'le teach her how to fight
And hold her weapon. Oh I laugh amaine,
To ſee the madnes of this *Martius* vaine.

    But roome for *Tuſcus*, that ieſt-mounging youth
Who nere did ope his Apiſh gerning mouth
But to retaile and broke anothers wit.
Diſcourſe of what you will, he ſtraight can fit
Your preſent talke, with, *Sir, I'le tell a ieſt*
(Of ſome ſweet Ladie, or graund Lord at leaſt)
Then on he goes, and nere his tongue ſhall lie
Till his ingroſſed ieſts are all drawne dry:
But then as dumbe as *Maurus*, when at play
Hath loſt his crownes, and paun'd his trim array.
He doth naught but retaile ieſts :∘ breake but one,
Out flies his table-booke; let him alone,
He'le haue it i-faith; Lad, haſt an Epigram,
Wilt haue it put into the chaps of Fame?
Giue *Tuſcus* copies ; ſooth, as his owne wit
(His proper iſſue) he will father it.
O that this Eccho, that doth ſeake, ſpet, write
Naught but the excrements of others ſpright,
This il-ſtuft trunke of ieſts (whoſe very ſoule
Is but a heape of libes) ſhould once inroule
His name 'mong creatures termed rationall!
Whoſe chiefe repute, whoſe ſenſe, whoſe ſoule and all
Are fed with offall ſcraps, that ſometimes fall
From liberall wits, in their large feſtiuall,

    Come aloft Iack, roome for a vaulting ſkip,
Roome for *Torquatus*, that nere op't his lip
But in prate of *pummado reuerſa*,
Of the nimbling tumbling *Angelica.*

U 2

Now on

Now on my soule, his very intellect
Is naught but a curuetting *Sommerset.*

   Hush, hush, (cries honest *Phylo*) peace, desist,
Dost thou not tremble sower Satyrist,
Now that iudiciall Musus readeth thee?
He'le whip each line he'll scourge thy balladry,
Good faith he will,   *Phylo* I pre thee stay
Whilst I the humour of this dogge display:
He's naught but censure, wilt thou credit me,
He neuer writ one line in poesie,
But once at Athens in a theame did frame
A paradox in praise of vertues name:
Which still he hugs, and luls as tenderly
As cuckold *Tisus* his wifes bastardie.
Well, here's a challange, I flatly say he lyes,
That heard him ought but censure poesies.
Tis his discourse, first hauing knit the brow,
Stroke vp his fore-top, champed euery row,
Belcheth his flauering censure on each booke
That dare presume euen on *Medusa* looke.

   I haue no Artists skill in symphonies,
Yet when some pleasing Diapason flies
From out the belly of a sweete tough't Lute,
My eares dare say tis good: or when they sute
Some harsher seauens for varietie.
My natiue skill discernes it presently,
What then? will any sottish dolt repute,
Or euer thinke me *Orpheus* absolute?
Shall all the world of Fidlers follow mee,
Relying on my voice in musickrie?
   Musus heere's *Rhodes*, lets see thy boasted leape,
Or els avaunt lewd curre, presume not speake,

                              Or with

Or with thy venome-fputtering chaps to barke
'Gainft well-pend poems, in the tongue-tied dark.
  O for a humour, looke who yon doth goe,
The meager lecher, lewd *Luxurio:*
Tis he that hath the fole monopoly
By patent, of the Superb lechery.
No newe edition of drabbes comes out,
But feene and allow'd by *Luxuries* fnout.
Did euer any man ere heare him talke
But of Pick-hatch, or of fome Shoreditch baulke
Aretines filth, or of his wandring whore,
Of fome *Cynidian*, or of *Tacedore,*
Of *Rufcus* nafty lothfome brothell rime,
That ftinks like *Aiax* froth, or muck-pit flime?
The news he tels you, is of fome newe flefh,
Lately brooke vp, fpan newe, hote piping frefh.
The curtefie he fhewes you, is fome morne
To giue you *Venus* fore his fmock be on.
His eyes, his tongue, his foule, his all is luft,
Which vengeance and confufion follow muft.
Out on this falt humour, letchers dropfie,
Fie, it doth foyle my chafter poefie.
  O fpruce! How now *Pifo, Aurelius* Ape,
What ftrange difguife, what new deformed fhape
Doth hold thy thoughts in contemplation?
Faith fay, what fafhion art thou thinking on?
A ftitcht Taffata cloake, a pair of flops,
Of Spanifh leather? O who heard his chops
Ere chew of ought, but of fome ftrange difguife?
This fafhion-mounger, each morne fore he rife
Contemplates fute fhapes, and once from out his bed,
He hath them ftraight full liuely portrayed.

U 3.

And then

And then he chukes, and is as proude of this
As *Taphus* when he got his neighbours bliffe.
All fashions since the first yeare of this Queene
May in his study fairely drawne be seene,
And all that shall be to his day of doome,
You may peruse within that little roome.
For not a fashion once dare show his face,
But from neat *Pyfo* first must take his grace.
The long fooles coat, the huge slop, the hugd boot
From mimick *Pyfo*, all doe claime their roote.
O that the boundlesse power of the soule
Should be coop't vp in fashioning some roule!

But O, *Suffenus*, (that doth hugge, imbrace
His proper selfe, admires his owne sweet face,
Prayseth his owne faire limmes proportion,
Kisseth his shade, recounteth all alone
His owne good parts) who envies him? not I,
For well he may, wishous all rivalrie.

Fie, whether's fled my sprites alacritie?
How dull I vent this humorous poesie!
In faith I am sad, I am possest with ruth,
To see the vainenesse of faire *Albions* youth;
To see their richest time euen wholly spent
In that which is but Gentries ornament,
Which being meanly done, becomes them well:
But when with deere times losse they doe excell,
How ill they doe things well! To daunce and sing,
To vault, to fence, and fairely trot a ring
With good grace, meanely done, O what repute
They doe beget! But being absolute,
It argues too much time, too much regard
Imploy'd in that which might be better spar'd

Then

Then fubftance fhould be loft,   If one fhould fewe
For *Lefbias* loue, hauing two daies to wooe
And not one more, and fhould imploy thofe twaine
The fauour of her wayting wench to gaine,
Were he not mad? Your apprehenfion:
Your wits are quick in application.

Gallants.

Me thinks your foules fhould grudge, and inly fcorn
To be made flaues, to humours that are borne
In flime of filthy fenfualitie.
That part, not fubiect to mortalitie
(Boundleffe, difcurfiue apprehenfion
Giuing it wings to act his function)
Me thinks fhould murmur, when you ftop his courfe,
And foyle his beauties in fome beaftly fource
Of brutifh pleafures. But it is fo poore,
So weake, fo hunger bitten, euermore
Kept from his foode, meager for want of meate,
Scorn'd and reiected, thruft from out his feate,
Vpbrai'd by Capons greace, confumed quite
By eating ftewes, that wafte the better fpright,
Snibd by his bafer parts; that now poore *Soule*
(Thus pefanted to each lewd thoughts controule)
Hath loft all heart, bearing all iniuries,
The vtmoft fpight, and rank'ft indignities
With forced willingneffe. Taking great ioy
If you will daine his faculties imploy
But in the mean'ft ingenious qualitie.
(How proud he'll be of any dignitie?)
Put it to mufick, dauncing, fencing fchoole,
Lord how I laugh to heare the prettie foole

How is

How it will prate! his tongue shall neuer lie,
But still discourse of his spruce qualitie;
Egging his master to proceede from this,
And get the substance of celestiall blisse.
His Lord straight cals his parliament of sence,
But still the sensuall haue preheminence.
The poore soules better part so feeble is,
So colde and dead is his *Synderesis*,
That shadowes by odde chaunce sometimes are got,
But O the substance is respected not.
Here ends my rage, though angry brow was bent,
Yet I haue sung in sporting merriment.

To euerlasting O B L I U I O N.

THOU mightie gulfe, insatiat cormorant,
    Deride me not, though I seeme petulant
To fall into thy chops. Let others pray
For euer their faire Poems flourish may.
But as for mee, hungry *Obliuion*
Deuour me quick, accept my orizon:
    My earnest prayers, which doe importune thee,
    With gloomy shade of thy still Emperie,
    To vaile both me and my rude poesie.
Farre worthier lines in silence of thy state
Doe sleepe securely free from loue or hate:
From which this liuing nere can be exempt,
But whilst it breathes will hate and furie tempt.
Then close his eyes with thy all-dimming hand,
Which not right glorious actions can with-stand.

Peace

Peace hatefull tongues, I now in silence pace,
Vnlesse fome hound doe wake me from my place,
   I with this fharpe, yet well meant poefie,
   Will fleepe fecure, right free from iniurie
   Of cancred hate, or rankeft villanie.

❀❀❀❀❀❀❀❀❀❀❀❀❀❀❀❀❀❀❀

To him that hath perufed mee.

GENTLE, or vngentle hand that holdeft mee, let
not thine eye be caft vpon priuateneffe, for I proteft I glaunce not on it. If thou haft perufed mee, what
leffer fauour canft thou grant then not to abufe mee with
vniuft application? Yet I feare mee, I fhall be much,
much iniured by two fortes of readers: the one being
ignorant, not knowing the nature of a Satyre, (which
is, vnder fained priuate names, to note generall vices,)
will needes wreft each fained name to a priuate vnfained
perfon. The other too fubtile, bearing a priuate ma-
lice to fome greater perfonage then hee dare in his owne
perfon feeme to maligne, will arife by a forced application of my generall reproofes to broach his priuate
hatred. Then the which I knowe not a greater iniury
can be offered to a Satyrift. I durft prefume, knew
they how guiltleffe, and how free I were from prying
into priuateneffe, they would them to thinke, how much
they wrong themfelues, in feeking to iniure mee. Let
this proteftation fatisfie our curious fearchers. So may I
obtaine my beft hopes, as I am free from endeauouring
to blaft anie priuate man's good name. If any one
(forced with his owne guilt) will turne it home and fay
                               Tis I,

Tis I, I can not hinder him.   Neither do I iniure him.
For other faults of Poefie, I craue no pardon, in that I
fcorne all pennance the bitterest cenfurer can impofe
vpon mee.   Thus (wifhing each man to leaue enquiring
who I am, and learne to knowe himfelfe,) I take a fo-
lemne congee of this fuftie world.

THERIOMASTIX.

F I N I S.

CPSIA information can be obtained
at www.ICGtesting.com
Printed in the USA
BVHW031410220519
549025BV00004B/21/P

9 781165 000845